VITRU
ARCHITECT AND
ENGINEER

Buildings and building techniques
in Augustan Rome

INSIDE THE ANCIENT WORLD

General Editor: M. R. F. Gunningham

Other titles in the series

Robin Barrow: *Athenian Democracy*
Robin Barrow: *Greek and Roman Education*
Kenneth McLeish: *Roman Comedy*
Massey and Moreland: *Slavery in Ancient Rome*
Meg Parker: *Socrates and Athens*
John Richardson: *Roman Provincial Administration*
John Sharwood Smith: *The Bride from the Sea*
David Taylor: *Cicero and Rome*
Martin Thorpe: *Homer*
Diana Topham-Meekings: *The Hollow Ships*
R. D. Williams: *Aeneas and the Roman Hero*

INSIDE THE ANCIENT WORLD

VITRUVIUS, ARCHITECT AND ENGINEER

Buildings and building techniques in Augustan Rome

ALEXANDER McKAY

MACMILLAN EDUCATION

First published 1978

Published by
MACMILLAN EDUCATION LTD
Houndmills Basingstoke Hampshire RG21 2XS and London
Associated companies in Delhi Dublin Hong Kong Johannesburg Lagos Melbourne New York Singapore and Tokyo

Filmset by Keyspools Ltd Golborne Lancs
Printed in Hong Kong by Bright Sun Printing Press Co. Ltd.

British Library Cataloguing in Publication Data
McKay, Alexander Gordon
Vitruvius, architect and engineer.
– (Inside the ancient world).
1. Vitruvius I. Series
720'.92'4 NA340.V5

ISBN 0–333–18319–3

Contents

Illustrations

Author's preface

Vitruvius was a practising architect, an arms expert and hydraulic engineer during the age of Caesar and Augustus. After two thousand years, his *Ten Books on Architecture* still offer valid advice on specifications, design, cost factors, functionalism, and aesthetics.

Vitruvius spent most of his professional life in the armed services. His somewhat doctrinaire, authoritarian style often recalls that of the army commander; there is the same concern for principles of strategy and tactics amidst scenes of crisis, confusion, and sometimes squalor; there is the same determination to apply saving principles in the face of difficulties.

How was this ancient Roman architect-engineer educated? What was the state of the profession which he entered? Who were the personalities who shaped the age and provided the patronage for his construction programmes? What was the Rome of Caesar and Augustus like? What were the most striking monuments and engineering achievements of the city and of the empire? What did Vitruvius contribute to the practice and the aesthetics of his contemporary architecture? These are just some of the questions which this book sets out to answer.

ALEXANDER G. McKAY

Acknowledgements

The author and publishers wish to acknowledge the following photograph and artwork sources:

Hirmer Verlag, Munich: cover
American School of Classical Studies, Athens: p. 62
Archive Fotogref, Vaticani: p. 16
British Library: p. 33
Cambridge University Press: p. 70
Fototeca Unione: pp. 42, 44, 46, 73
A.F. Kersting: p. 34
Metropolitan Museum of Art: p. 63
Museo della Civittà Romana: pp. 15, 23
Museo Nazionale, Napoli: p. 65
Musei, Vaticani: p. 53

The publishers have made every effort to trace the copyright holders, but if they have inadvertently overlooked any, they will be pleased to make the necessary arrangements at the earliest opportunity.

I

The author and the profession

Vitruvius' career

The life-span of Vitruvius seems to have encompassed sixty or so years of the last century BC, one of the most exciting eras of Rome's history.

In the preface to his most famous work, *De Architectura*, a treatise on architecture and engineering, he acknowledges his debt to his parents for their concern about his education:

I am infinitely grateful to my parents because they approved of the law of Athens and were concerned that I should be taught my art, one which cannot be brought to perfection without learning and a liberal education in all branches of knowledge. [6. Pref. 4]

Private means and patronage probably freed Vitruvius from the necessity (or the desire) to acquire a fortune. As he himself says:

For my part, Caesar, I have never been zealous about acquiring money from my profession, but have maintained that modest means and a good reputation are a better pursuit than wealth and notoriety. For that reason I have only a modest reputation. . . . Other architects request and canvass for commissions; but I have been trained by my masters to accept a commission only after being asked, and never to request one. [6. Pref. 5]

Specific details about Vitruvius' engineering career have to be gleaned from his treatise. While campaigning in the Maritime Alps in 58–57 BC, Caesar encountered a fire-resistant wood (larch) during the siege of Larignum's walls. Vitruvius, evidently an eye-witness to its properties, comments on its use in north-western Italy, and even speculates on its advantages as a protection against tenement fires in the capital [2. 9. 15–16]. On another occasion he discusses the properties of water and other subjects with Gaius Julius Masintha (Masinissa). This Numidian prince was a favourite of Caesar's who enjoyed the latter's protection in Africa and accompanied him to Spain in 60 BC [Suetonius, *Caesar* 71]. Vitruvius may have conversed with Masintha either in Spain or in Africa (during Caesar's campaign at Thapsus in 46 BC).

Vitruvius' career as architect-engineer under Caesar was no doubt advanced by his success as an arms expert.

> Marcus Aurelius, Publius Minidius, and Gnaeus Cornelius and I were assigned the construction and repair of *ballistae*, *scorpiones*, and other artillery pieces and with them I have received rewards for my service. [1. Pref. 2]

Vitruvius, and his three colleagues, must have formed part of the technical company of architects, surveyors and engineers involved in Caesar's military exploits and post-war settlements. Encampments, war machines, naval construction, brick-making, carpentry, pile-bridges, surveying, roads, canals, harbours, forts and walls, were but a few of the demands made of the architect-technician in the Roman legions.

Vitruvius' awareness of building materials, constructions and local peculiarities in Hither and Further Spain, Gaul, Cisalpine Gaul, Greece (particularly Athens) and Asia Minor are probably the combined product of his experience with Julius Caesar and of diligent tourism. The source books to which he alludes also provided him with classical references and other details of general interest.

After Caesar's assassination in 44 BC, Vitruvius transferred his loyalty to the young Octavian (who took the name Augustus, after his victory at Actium, in 27 BC). He no doubt continued to serve as an artillery expert during the Second Triumvirate of Octavian, Mark Antony, and Lepidus. During the early Principate of Augustus, although Vitruvius probably contributed some of the strategic weaponry for Agrippa's naval and land offensive against Sextus Pompey, the freedman L. Cocceius Auctus captured the limelight for his resourceful and prodigious undertakings in the Cumaean zone. On the other hand, Octavia, sister of the Princeps and wife of Mark Antony, showed Vitruvius special favour [1. Pref. 2].

His engineering capabilities were certainly enlisted by M. Vipsanius Agrippa during his tenure of office as *curator aquarum publicarum* (see page24). Vitruvius seems to have initiated the use of a newly-designed lead pipe (*quinarius*) which assisted Agrippa's extensive repairs and innovations to the water-supply system of the capital. Although he may have been involved in several of the monumental projects of the age, his name can be attached specifically to only one urban scheme – the forum of the Augustan colony at Fanum Fortunae (modern Fano) in Umbria. The account of his design of the law-court or basilica, his use of material and skilful techniques, illuminate his expertise as designer and builder [5. 1. 6–10]. His basilica, which has never been located with certainty, rose at one short end of an elongated rectangular piazza. A large central door provided access from the central line of the forum and opened into the high horizontal hall of the law-court extending symmetrically to right and left. The short axis was aligned with the centre of a recess (*exedra*) containing a sanctuary of Augustus. At the opposite end of the piazza towered the temple of Jupiter, the Capitolium of the colony. Colonnades along the flanks of the forum united the dominant structures and framed the civic centre.

During his later years and period of retirement Vitruvius was appointed, and reappointed, by Augustus to a military surveyorship (*recognitio*) and received, it appears, a life pension from the same source [I. Pref. 2 & 3].

The profession

There can have been no lack of architects during the last century of the Roman Republic. Cicero, whose town and country mansions made heavy demands on architects' skills and patience, paid a compliment to the profession:

Skills which require greater intelligence or utility, like medicine, architecture, or the teaching of rhetoric, are honourable for those to whose social class they are appropriate. [Cicero, *De Officiis* 1. 151]

Elsewhere, we find a cynical account of his interview with a Greek-speaking slave professional who had been instructed to enlarge the size of his library's windows:

When I spoke to Cyrus he told me that views on to a garden through wide windows were less attractive – for let the eye be A, the visible objects B and C, and the light-rays D and F. . . . You know the rest. [Cicero, *Ad Q.F.* 2, 2]

Vitruvius had no misgivings about the status of the profession and he was adamant about the necessity for a liberal education. The architect

should also be a man of letters, an expert draughtsman, a mathematician familiar with scientific thought, a painstaking student of philosophy, acquainted with music, not ignorant of medicine, knowledgeable about the opinions of jurists, and familiar with astronomy and the theory of the heavens. [1. 1. 3]

The product of such an extensive and liberal curriculum was an architect in the true sense and as was implied by the title *archi-tectus*, something more than 'master-builder'. The accumulation of such a vast range of subject matter required the aspiring architect to begin with service as apprentice to some master artist. Study of philosophy would provide a spur to high-minded modesty and honesty; musical training would enable him to tune *ballistae*, catapults and *scorpiones* with better success, and ensure proper acoustics in theatres; study of medicine would direct the choice of hygienic town sites; legal training would help to ensure the drafting of fair contracts; and astronomy, rather unexpectedly, would assist the proper design of sun-dials!

Draughtsmanship was, naturally, a basic necessity. Vitruvius indicates that plans, elevations, perspective views and coloured renderings (on stone, terracotta tile, marble, mosaic or ephemeral papyrus) were basic to the exercise:

Plans demand competent use of compass and ruler, and with these the correct designs are made on the sites. Elevation is the vertical likeness of the facade, a slightly shaded drawing which outlines the finished appearance. Perspective also is the shading of the facade, and of the retreating sides, with all of the lines converging at a point which is the centre of a circle. [1. 2. 2]

Other advantages attach to the curriculum:

An architect must be literate so as to keep a lasting record of precedents. By his expertise in draughtsmanship he will find it easy by coloured drawings to illustrate the desired effect. Mathematics also offers many advantages for the architect. It teaches the use of ruler and compass, and so simplifies the layout of buildings on their locations by the use of set-squares, levels, and alignments. By optics, in the case of buildings, light may be derived from certain quarters of the sky. By arithmetic one may assess the cost of a building; the methods of measurement are indicated; and the tricky problems of symmetry are solved by geometrical rules and methods. [1. 1. 4]

Contemporary standards and practice

The building mania of his century, inspired by generals competing with easy money against one another in the domain of architecture, and by the demands of wealthy freedmen, prompted many to enter the architectural profession and to strive recklessly for fame, multiple commissions, and a rich return. Property-owners, in Vitruvius' view, are less discriminating in their choice of architects, and the old criteria have been lost:

> Our ancestors used to give commissions in the first place to architects with a decent background and then inquired whether they had been liberally educated. They believed that one should rely on the honour of a gentleman rather than on impudent flashiness. The practitioners themselves used to instruct only their own sons or relatives, and trained them to be morally upright persons who could be trusted without hesitation in matters of such financial importance. [6. Pref. 6]

Mamurra, Caesar's chief engineer and aide, amassed a great fortune from the campaigns in Spain and Gaul. The immorality and extravagance of this man from Formiae were notorious, but he was a highly successful and experienced engineer. Nowadays, Vitruvius complains, the profession has been degraded by unattractive, inadequately-trained individuals:

> When I observe that this magnificent profession is light-heartedly practised by uneducated and inexperienced men, who, far from being familiar with architecture, are ignorant even of the carpenter's trade, I have only praise for those property owners who, confident in their learning, are courageous enough to build for themselves. . . . Their judgement is that, if they must rely on inexperienced persons, it is more appropriate for them to spend their capital according to their own desires rather than follow those of a stranger. [6. Pref. 6]

Vitruvius makes no platform attack on contemporary luxury and conspicuous consumption, but he is critical of the expense involved in the use of costly marbles and he lays down a peremptory law:

An architect should not request materials which cannot be supplied and processed without great outlay. [1. 2. 8]

BUILDING REGULATIONS

Vitruvius refers to the legal code of Ephesus, a city of Asia Minor, which requires the architect to conform with the building regulations and to provide guarantees and careful preliminary estimates in connection with public works projects [10. Pref. 1]. The Ephesian architects were personally responsible for all costs exceeding twenty-five per cent of their total estimates. The faults of his own 'generation of vipers' in the architectural profession induced Vitruvius to invoke the immortal gods:

If only the everlasting Gods had made this a law of the Roman people, also, not only for public, but also for private buildings . . . Citizens of some means would not be seduced into endless and lavish expenditure, even to eviction from their properties, and the architects themselves would be compelled, through dread of the penalty, to be more careful in estimating and stating the projected cost, so that gentlemen would finish their buildings for the estimated sum, or with only a small supplement. [10. Pref. 2]

BUILDING PROCEDURES

During Republican times, the aediles let contracts to freedmen and private individuals; the contractor (*redemptor*) provided the workmen or slave gangs. Such contracts were controlled by the State which had to give them final approval. However, laws and regulations relating to building practice and safety measures were noticeably absent at Rome. Building laws mostly tended to concern religious property; some related to the thickness of walls and prohibited the use of wooden roof tiles. A remarkable number of houses collapsed during later Republican and Imperial times. Contractors evidently failed to heed one principle which Vitruvius records when they erected insecure apartment towers:

Public statutes do not permit a thickness of more than half a metre for party walls; but other walls are also erected of the same thickness lest the space be narrowed excessively. Brick walls of half a metre – not more than two or three bricks thick – cannot support more than a single-storeyed building. [2.8.17]

*1 Apartment house (*insula*) and arcade, Ostia, Imperial date*

Augustus showed concern for the accident-prone flats: the speech of a Republican architect, Rutilius' *On the height of buildings*, was read by him to the Senate [Suetonius, *Augustus* 89. 2]. With an eye no doubt to the high density zones and ghettoes where the poor congregated – the Aventine and Caelian Hills, the Argiletum and the Subura – Augustus limited the height of tenements to just over twenty metres [Strabo 5. 3. 7]. But the Augustan law affected only the street fronts; the courtyards and side-street wings might reach for the stars! And the top floors, where wooden construction was commonest, were virtual fire traps, hardly accessible to firefighters. The collapse of the roof would cause the skyscraper to tumble into the narrow streets, creating great havoc and confusion. Building contractors under Nero (AD 54–68) continued to use less expensive sun-dried brick instead of burnt brick for their four- to six-storey tenements. The great fire of AD 64 suggested that radical changes in the construction and the design of tenements were required.

The dedication to Augustus

Vitruvius' overall view of classical/Hellenistic ideas and practices and Roman adaptation and invention is entirely in accord with Roman experience generally. The pursuit of models, of examples of excellence, led the Roman artist inevitably to Greece. The respected

2 *C. Julius Caesar Octavianus Augustus*

norms, imbued with the idealism, perfection and rationalism which the Augustan age craved after generations of chaos and civil war, lay in the Greek world. Vitruvius, in the course of his treatise, seeks examples which both suggest and embody decorum and authority for Roman designers and builders. He dedicates his work circa 24 BC to his patron Augustus, as the Roman poets Horace and Vergil dedicated their works to Maecenas:

Because I observed that you have built and are now building extensively, and that you will exercise care in the future that our public and private buildings shall be a heritage to posterity with your other proud achievements, I have composed specific rules to enable you, by consulting them, to be personally aware of the quality both of existing works and of those still to be constructed. [1. Pref. 3]

Although dedicated to the Princeps, the treatise was meant to be primarily a handbook for architects and engineers; to supply standards of design and construction, past and present, as well as for military specialists, men in private practice, and civil servants.

2

A Roman treatise for Romans

Experience and wide reading guided Vitruvius. His written sources were Greek and consisted almost entirely of specialist commentaries on particular buildings, monographs on technical problems, or systems of proportion and the like. Vitruvius conceives his source-books (forty-two of them are named) in contemporary terms, for Augustan writers cultivated models and sought to become exemplars for their Roman successors: Vergil was Rome's Theocritus, Hesiod, and Homer; Horace was Rome's Archilochus and Alcaeus; Propertius was Rome's Callimachus. Vitruvius may have sought to become Rome's Hermogenes, the celebrated Hellenistic architect of the second century BC whose mastery of Ionic forms and proportions affected Vitruvius' account and influenced contemporary building designs in Rome. Hermogenes, like Vitruvius, left writings about his architectural works and theories. At any rate Vitruvius followed tradition when he presented his treatise to Augustus, as earlier practitioners of his art dedicated their works to Alexander or to his Hellenistic successors:

> I do not present a treatise in which the titles of other men's works and authorities have been suppressed and my name inserted, nor has it been my design to seek approval by criticising the opinions of anyone. On the contrary, I express infinite thanks to all authors who have compiled from antiquity noteworthy examples of the skill shown by genius and so provided us with copious materials of different sorts. I have drawn from them as men draw water from springs, and for their personal use, and have made my powers of writing more eloquent and less complicated. Relying on such authorities, I found the courage to put together new systems of instruction.
> [7. Pref. 10]

Vitruvius' use of the wellspring image recalls his career as a celebrated hydraulic engineer; it also marks an innocent, self-effacing insertion of himself into the array of experienced masters and theorists, who supplied many of his facts. His list of sources is overwhelmingly Greek. But there were some Roman exponents too: Fufidius, who first published on the topic, P. Terentius Varro (116–27 BC) and Publius Septimius. [7. Pref. 14]

Vitruvius was naturally sensitive to the enormous contribution of Greek architects to his profession; he was also, no doubt, depressed by the meagre Roman offering, a factor which prompted him to compose his treatise in order to restore the balance for the future. He had no doubts about the contribution of Roman architects to the evolutionary process. Both Cossutius and Gaius Mucius claim special mention but there are others, mute and unsung:

Cossutius (who applied the finishing touches to the Temple of Olympian Zeus in Athens) has left no commentary. ... Gaius Mucius, relying on his considerable experience, completed the *cella*, columns, and entablature of the Marian Temple of Honour and Valour, a modular design in accordance with the legitimate rules of the art. If this building had used marble so that besides its technical precision it displayed the prestige which comes from magnificence and costly outlay, it would be numbered among the foremost and greatest buildings. [7. Pref. 17]

Vitruvius meant to supply a systematic treatise which would break the conspiracy of silence about Roman practice:

Since we find that our pioneer architects, and a good many in our own day, have been as great as their counterparts, but that only a few of them have published handbooks, I thought that I should not remain silent but should treat the different topics methodically in separate books. [7. Pref. 18]

The art of architecture

Between the death of Julius Caesar and the death of Augustus (44 BC–AD 14), Rome saw approximately 127 important buildings constructed or restored. Vitruvius witnessed and perhaps participated in this impressive programme of public works in the capital.

Certainly he tried to communicate to Augustus, and to contemporary architects, some precise ideas about the ideal types of various buildings and about suitable materials. His concern was to have structures which would be appropriate to their situation and their function, which would be suitably ornamented and have an innate visual dignity.

Vitruvius is a traditionalist by nature, anxious to save the old forms, ready to revive their 'republican' virtues with superimposed Hellenistic refinements and marble adornment. His doctrinaire attitude includes an architectural 'philosophy' as well. He tries to categorise the 'reasonings' behind the profession – the *rationes disciplinae* – in as complete and logical a fashion as possible. He confesses his failings as a thinker, rhetorician and *grammaticus*, but he does claim some measure of originality for his undertaking [7. Pref. 15, 18]. He distinguishes the 'art', the designing ability of the *architectus*, from the aesthetic qualities of the product. The first, which is integral to the profession, consists in ordering specifications (*ordinatio*), proper design of forms (*designatio*), and allocation of costs (*distributio*); the second requires 'beauty and fitness', rhythm in the visual aspect (*eurhythmia*), a common scale of measure or 'module' (*symmetria*), and finally a formal functionalism, the appropriate use of styles and orders (*decor*). The last is particularly appropriate to the Augustan concept of 'architecture as message'.

In a manner which is polite, modest, circumspect and congenial, Vitruvius offers himself as an example, and encourages others to inject decorum and authority into Roman buildings. His success cannot be measured fairly; the bulk of Augustan building has perished, and we cannot be certain about his impact on Julio-Claudian builders.

THE CONTENTS OF THE TREATISE

Book One describes the education of the architect and the basic principles of the art, with some practical applications to city planning, walls, streets, and public buildings; *Book Two* examines Roman building materials; *Books Three* and *Four* examine religious architecture and the four orders (Doric, Ionic, Corinthian and Tuscan) with some discussion of theoretical problems attached to the layout and proportions of Greek temples; *Book Five* deals with public architecture (civic square, basilica, treasury buildings, prison, senate house, theatre, colonnades and walks, baths, palaestra, harbours, breakwaters, and shipyards); *Book Six* treats domestic architecture (town and country) and *Book Seven* deals with their interior decoration, stucco-work and murals; *Book Eight* is concerned with hydraulic engineering; *Book Nine* deals with astronomy, sun-dials and waterclocks; and *Book Ten* treats machinery, especially military engines, and includes hoisting devices, waterwheels and watermills, water-screw, pumps, water organ, and hodometer (distance measurer). The medley befits his own experience as civil and military engineer: the conception is surprisingly grand. Architecture, for Vitruvius, is concerned with the entire man-made environment, with man's manipulation of natural materials and forces, and with the laws that govern man and nature. His treatise may worthily be called the primer of the Art of Architecture.

3
From adobe to marble

The imperial facade

Vitruvius is remarkably close-lipped about Augustan buildings: Augustus himself was far less reticent. When he died in AD 14 he left behind 'a catalogue' of his achievements, the *Res Gestae*, which he wished to be inscribed on bronze tablets and mounted in front of his mausoleum beside the Tiber in Rome's Campus Martius. The best extant copy is inscribed on the walls of the Temple of Rome and Augustus in Ankara, Turkey. Its main intention is to evoke an image of the 'First Citizen' who, adhering strictly to constitutional means, redeemed the world from chaos and restored the Roman commonwealth. Augustus' building programme is an important facet of his image and accomplishment; the catalogue of his chief public works is meant not only to underline his liberality but to commemorate also his role as Pater Patriae (Father of his Country) and builder in his own right. During the reign of Hadrian (AD 117–138), Suetonius records that prior to the Principate 'the city was not adorned in proportion to the greatness of the empire and was subject to floods and fires: Augustus so beautified it that he justly boasted that he had found it made of adobe (sun-dried brick) and left it made of marble' [*Augustus* 28]. Augustus, and his advisers, obviously meant to create an imperial art and architecture. Vitruvius was part of this revolution of ideas in architecture. He sought, like Augustus, to encourage a new grandeur, dignity, nobility, and restraint in contemporary architecture; his formulations, often conservative, were to be the basis for subsequent elaboration.

THE PROGRAMME OF AUGUSTUS

'I built the Senate House and the Chalcidicum (porch) which adjoins it, the Temple of Apollo on the Palatine with its colonnades, the

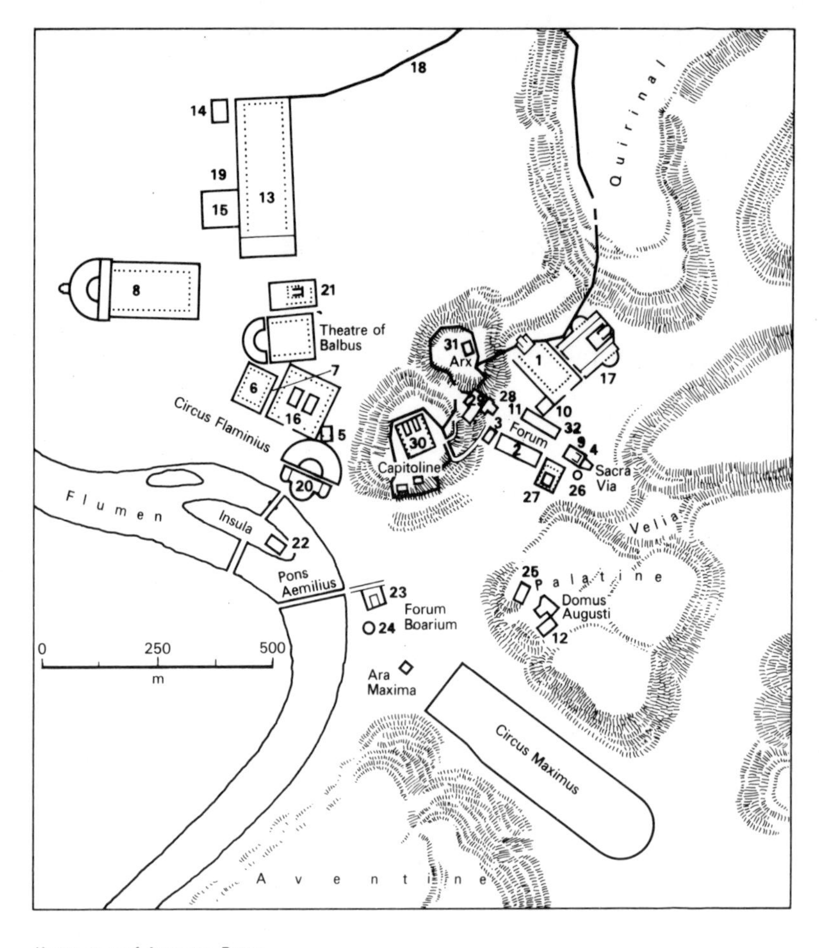

Key to map of Augustan Rome

1	Forum Julium, Temple of Venus Genetrix	17	Forum of Augustus, Temple of Mars Ultor
2	Basilica Julia	18	Aqua Virgo
3	Temple of Saturn	19	Stagnum
4	Regia	20	Theatre of Marcellus
5	Temple of Apollo Medicus	21	Porticus Minucia (granary)
6	Porticus Philippi	22	Temple of Aesculapius
7	Temple of Hercules Musarum	23	Temple of 'Fortuna Virilis' (Portunus)
8	Theatre and Porticus of Pompey	24	Temple of 'Vesta' (Hercules Victor)
9	Temple of Deified Julius	25	Temple of Magna Mater (Cybele)
10	Curia Julia	26	Temple of Vesta
11	Rostra	27	Temple of Castor and Pollux
12	Temple of Apollo Palatinus	28	Temple of Concord
13	Saepta Julia	29	Tabularium
14	Pantheon	30	Temple of Jupiter Capitolinus
15	Baths of Agrippa	31	Temple of Juno Moneta
16	Porticus Octaviae	32	Basilica Aemilia

3 The centre of Rome in the Augustan Age

Temple of the Deified Julius, the Lupercal, the colonnade near the Circus of Flaminius which I allowed to be called the Porticus Octaviae after the Octavius who built the previous portico on the same location, the imperial box (*pulvinar*) in the Circus Maximus, the temples on the Capitoline of Jupiter Feretrius and Jupiter Tonans (the Thunderer), the Temple of Quirinus, the Temples of Minerva, Juno Regina, and Jupiter Libertas on the Aventine, the Temple of the Lares at the summit of the Sacred Way, the Temple of the Penates on the Velia, the Temple of Youth, and the Temple of the Great Mother (Cybele) on the Palatine. I repaired the Capitol and the Theatre of Pompey, both at great expense, without inscribing my name. I repaired the water conduits of the aqueducts, which in numerous places were disintegrating through age, and I doubled the flow of the Marcian aqueduct by connecting it to a new source. I completed the Forum Julium and the Basilica (Julia) between the Temples of Castor and Saturn, an edifice begun and partly completed by my father, after it had been destroyed by fire. I began to rebuild it on a larger site under the names of my sons (Gaius and Lucius) and in case I do not complete it during my lifetime, I have ordered my heirs to finish it. During my sixth consulship (28 BC) I repaired eighty-two temples of the gods within the city at the instigation of the Senate and passed over none that needed repairs at that time. In my seventh consulship I repaired the Flaminian Highway from Rome as far as Ariminum,

4 *The Theatre of Marcellus, Rome*

together with all the bridges except the Mulvian and the Minucian. I built from the spoils of war the Temple of Mars the Avenger and the Forum of Augustus on ground which I personally owned. I built the theatre adjacent to the Temple of Apollo on land mostly purchased from private owners and provided that it should bear the name of Marcus Marcellus, my son-in-law.' [*Res Gestae Divi Augusti* 19–21]

The catalogue, though impressive, is incomplete; for example, it omits the Mausoleum Augusti where the testament was exhibited and the flanking obelisks at the entrance. The Augustan list actually includes only monuments for which the Princeps assumed responsibility. There were others, voted by the Senate, in the shape of altars and triumphal arches, and additional constructions by the friends of Augustus and prominent aristocrats: the Pantheon (M. Agrippa), the Atrium Libertatis (Gaius Asinius Pollio), the Regia (Gnaeus Domitius Calvinus), the Porticus Philippi and Temple of Hercules Musarum (L. Marcius Philippus), the Temple of Diana on the Aventine (L. Cornificius), and the first stone amphitheatre in Rome (T. Statilius Taurus).

The scale of the building operations is staggering, the cost immense. There were several important incentives to the programme. The devastation of civil war, of earthquake, fire and flood, were formidable; the temples, and no doubt much of the civic architecture, had been unavoidably neglected during the war years; stucco facings and decorative finishing must have suffered badly. The flood of immigrants into the city during the civil wars and after the peace, increased the population to approximately 750 000 and the demands for housing and for public utilities put a great strain on the existing resources. To provide extra public accommodation and improved services, and to ensure better security, the building programme was sheer necessity. The opportunities for employment which the programme afforded to skilled and unskilled labour, free and servile, in other words to the employable proletariate of the capital, was a godsend to civic pride and the general welfare.

M. Vipsanius Agrippa, Augustus' military aide and later son-in-law, was surpassed only by the Princeps in his building operations. As aedile, Agrippa built the Julian aqueduct in 33 BC, bringing to five the number of aqueducts which provided Rome with water. Because the maintenance of the city's aqueducts had proved inadequate and inefficient when left to private contractors, Augustus entrusted their supervision to Agrippa as *curator aquarum publicarum*. A gang of two hundred and forty slaves was organised and trained to cope with routine duties. Vitruvius was probably working alongside Agrippa as a hydraulic engineer when he adapted his lead pipe measurement (*quinarius*). Thanks to Agrippa, the populace could depend on a constant water supply in the public fountains. Sanitation and public health also improved. Rome's water supply and refuse disposal were closely linked and Agrippa's construction of the Aqua Julia was complemented by the systematic cleaning of the city sewers. Public latrines enjoyed an uninterrupted flow of water and the city's sewers were the receptacles for street refuse and litter. Agrippa also provided storerooms and shopping facilities in the centre of the city. The new warehouse, called the Horrea Agrippiana, serviced small shopkeepers and tradesmen, particularly clothiers, south of the Forum Romanum.

Fire and flood

FIRE FIGHTING

Fire protection scarcely existed in the Republican metropolis and devastating fires were common. Some people profited by the recurrent disasters. Marcus Licinius Crassus would appear at the scene and bargain for the property and the neighbouring buildings which seemed endangered, offering an absurdly low price. After his slaves, part of a corps of five hundred, trained as construction workers, had extinguished the flames and razed the buildings, Crassus had houses or tenements constructed on the site. Real estate holdings and rentals provided rich returns for him.

Vitruvius [10. 7. 1] describes a water pump (*sipho*), invented by Ctesibius the Alexandrian; it consisted basically of two pistons in two cylinders which forced the water from a reservoir or street fountain upwards through a pipe. The device must surely have served as a fire-fighting device before Vitruvius' time. Vitruvius refers to constructional devices rather than external aids:

If only there were easy transit for this material (larchwood) to Rome, it would be extraordinarily serviceable in buildings; perhaps not for general purposes, but if the boards used in the eaves of house blocks were made of it, the buildings would escape the threat of fire spreading across to them, because larch boards can neither catch fire from flames or from burning coals, nor ignite spontaneously. [2. 9. 16]

Because efforts to improve on private vigilance against fires were fruitless, Augustus gave the aediles in 23 BC a corps of six hundred slaves as a public fire department. Finally, in AD 6, Augustus moved even more decisively against the problem and established a corps of professional firemen (*vigiles*) organised into seven cohorts, each containing one thousand men, and commanded by tribunes; the *praefectus vigilum*, of equestrian rank, was directly responsible to the Princeps.

THE MENACE OF FLOODS

Floods were always a menace during the winter rains and the springtime torrents from the mountainous hinterland of the capital. The inundation of 54 BC covered the lower-lying sectors of the city and even advanced into the upper areas. Numerous adobe buildings (see page 38), both houses and apartments, collapsed because they were undermined and impregnated by the floodwaters. Julius Caesar devised a scheme to divert the Tiber into a new channel which would start at the Mulvian Bridge, run along the foot of Monte Mario, then, in all likelihood, rejoin the old river-bed near the Castle Sant'Angelo. But the dictator's death stopped the projected channel improvement and Augustus did not pursue the project. Floods indeed remained a cause for anxiety among the citizens until the twentieth century.

4

Building programmes at home and abroad

Rome

BUILDINGS IN THE CAMPUS MARTIUS

Agrippa's efforts as water administrator resulted in extensive repairs to the aqueducts, new construction (the Aqua Julia, 19 BC), and improved drainage; he also built seven hundred basins, five hundred fountains, and one hundred and thirty distribution points, all embellished with hundreds of bronze and marble statues and marble columns. But his most impressive and popular construction was the complex of buildings in the Campus Martius.

Strabo, the Greek geographer, provides an eyewitness reaction to the dazzling array and organised space of the ancient meeting-place of the Roman assemblies. Pompey's Theatre (55–52 BC), the first element, remained the focus of popular attention and the spur to Julian projects:

Pompey and the Deified Caesar, Augustus and his sons, his friends and wife and sister, have surpassed all others in their zeal for buildings and in the expense incurred. The Campus Martius contains most of these and so, in addition to its natural amenities, it has undergone a process of calculated adornment. The area of the Campus is remarkable, it provides space at the same time, and with no interference, for chariot-racing and every conceivable equestrian exercise, as well as for crowds of people who exercise themselves by playing ball, by rolling hoops, and by wrestling; the works of art installed around the Campus, the grounds, which are grass-covered throughout the year, and the summits of the hills which rise above the river and extend to its banks, present to the eye the appearance of a painted stage-set all of which, I maintain, affords a spectacle from which it is difficult to tear oneself away. Most eye-catching is the so-called Mausoleum, a sizeable mound beside the Tiber set on a high foundation of white marble, densely planted with evergreens to the summit. A bronze likeness of Augustus Caesar stands on top; behind the tumulus is a spacious sacred precinct with marvellous walks. [Strabo 5. 3. 8]

Strabo gives the impression that architects and landscape designers were united in the urban project:

There are colonnades in considerable numbers, sacred precincts, three theatres and an amphitheatre, and very costly temples, one after another in close succession which suggests that they are trying, so to speak, to declare the rest of the city a mere appendage. [ibid.]

Here the city-dweller, freed from his shop or tenement cubicle, could find endless vistas of clean facades, public baths, theatres, a race course, a gladiatorial arena, exercise grounds, and parkland. The crushing anonymity, loneliness and unsightliness of the high-rise apartments (*insulae*) could be escaped and forgotten in this splendid new sector where one-time military and political activities gradually gave place to less taxing diversions.

THE ROMAN FORUM

The ancient civic centre, hallowed by time and historical events, marred by civil strife and deliberate destruction, cried out for improvement and alignment with the new political scene. The Forum, in Vitruvius' lifetime, was a conglomeration of monuments and streets, an environment for human activity, political, mercantile and judicial. The ancient temples, many of them in desperate condition and neglected by worshippers, were in serious need of repair and reconstruction. The programme of 28 BC must have coped with some of the disrepair; friends of Augustus applied saving measures to others.

Julius Caesar had made enormous strides towards reorganising the motley collection of buildings by removing the old Rostra and the Basilica Porcia which had enclosed the old assembly place (Comitium). In the year of his death, Caesar relocated the Rostra, the speaker's platform, where it stands today, and the Senate House (Curia) along the northern edge of the Forum. He also set a precedent for Augustus by encouraging wealthy aristocrats and associates to improve and embellish older monuments. The Basilica Aemilia, opposite his still incomplete Basilica Julia, was sheathed in marble, and L. Munatius Plancus (who later proposed that Octavian be called Augustus), converted the Temple of Saturn from travertine (see page 37) to marble, suggesting a process which Octavian pursued himself with unparalleled extravagance in 28 BC. The Record Office (Tabularium), begun by Sulla and completed by C. Lutatius Catulus (78 BC), provided an open arcade as backdrop to the Republican Forum beneath the Capitoline slopes.

By 34 BC, thanks to Octavian's pious support, the Temple of the Deified Julius had risen on the spot where Caesar's corpse had been cremated after Antony's funeral oration. A speaker's platform, a metre high, stood in front of the temple, replacing the older Tribunal Aurelium, and faced west; beaks (*rostra*) from the ships captured at Actium adorned its facade. The new Rostra marked a shift in gravity in the civic centre, from the northern to the southern 'Julian' zone. The Senate voted to raise a triumphal arch between the Temple of Divus Julius and Castor's Temple to honour Octavian's victory at Actium. The triumphal passageway bore a simple, eloquent Attic inscription: 'For the Preservation of the State'. The arch was superseded, in 19 BC, by a more elaborate triple arch, a little further to

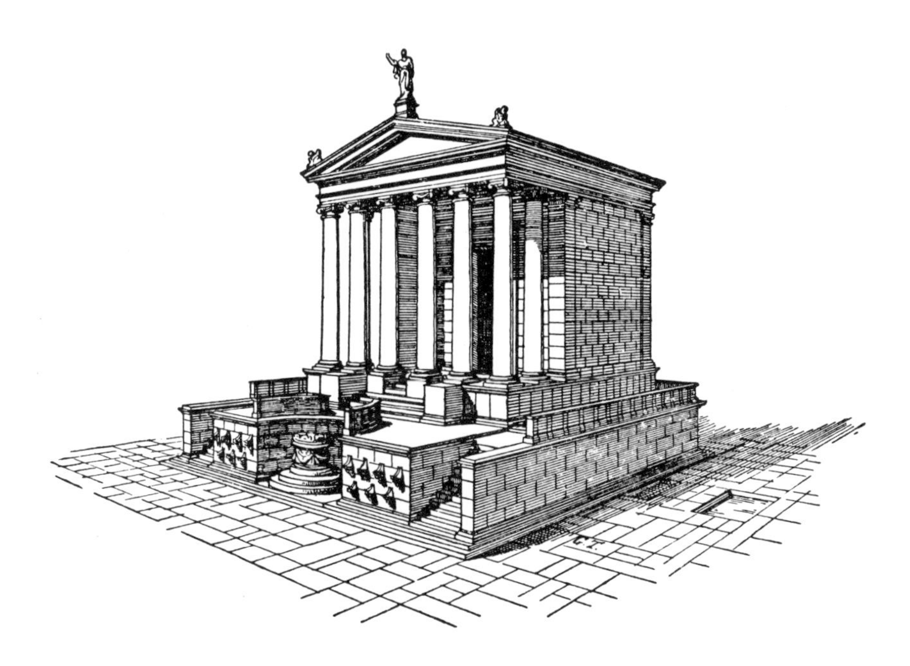

5 *Temple of the Deified Julius, Roman Forum*

the east, which celebrated Augustus' recovery by diplomacy rather than by force of arms of the Roman prisoners and military standards lost to the Parthians.

Vitruvius witnessed the emergence of a dynastic complex of buildings in the ancient civic square: the temple would remind Romans that Augustus was *Divi Filius*, son of a deified mortal, whose ancestry reached back to Aeneas and Venus; the Rostra were a reminder of the war to end all wars at Actium; and the single arch expressed the State's gratitude to the Princeps for its salvation.

Augustus' own contributions to the Forum were many. The Senate House, burnt down during riots in 52 BC, was redesigned as the Curia Julia by Caesar. Augustus completed the building, lodged in its interior a gilt-bronze statue of Victory, and added a courtyard for the storage of documents (the so-called Chalcidicum) behind the Senate House. He also completed the Basilica Julia, which Caesar had begun on the site of the earlier Basilica Sempronia; the 'old shops' (*tabernae veteres*) were given new shelter in the galleries of the arcade which opened on to the Forum. Minor repairs must have been made to other temples and shrines in the area during Octavian's sixth consulship (28 BC). Gnaeus Domitius Calvinus rebuilt or restored the Regia in marble.

THE FORUM OF JULIUS CAESAR

Caesar's architectural additions and alterations to the Forum Romanum adhered to the pattern set by the Dictator Sulla. Both men sought to win popular favour by providing the Romans with a centre where they could play their roles, major or minor, in a grandiose sculptured space. Certainly Augustus was their heir although he sought to confirm his prestige and position (*auctoritas*) by supplanting, in some measure, the embarrassing Republican accents in favour of visible testimony to the new ideology and the classical pattern of his regime.

Caesar's Forum behind the Curia Julia marked a new departure. Here for the first time, was visible propaganda in support of the Dictator and his family. The construction programme answered a vow made before the victory over Pompey at Pharsalus (48 BC). A recently-discovered inscription, on the obelisk in the piazza of the Basilica of St Peter in Rome, reveals that C. Cornelius Gallus, Rome's first elegiac poet and later prefect of Egypt, completed the Forum in his capacity as chief engineer of Octavian. The square incorporated a Temple of Venus Genetrix at its western extremity. The Corinthian temple, mounted on a high cement podium dressed with marble, was lavishly decorated with a frieze of cupids and colourful interior walls of marble; the apsidal (possibly vaulted) cella, housed the cult statue of Venus, a statue of Caesar, a gilded bronze statue of Cleopatra, and priceless paintings. The long, narrow piazza, 160 metres by seventy-five, was enclosed on three sides by a double-storeyed colonnade. The temple, which dominated the square, recalled Hellenistic sanctuaries of deified rulers. Venus, richly accommodated, and the opening ceremony, with Caesar seated before the temple on high, underlined the Dictator's impressive design. Vitruvius [3. 3. 2] refers to the closely-set columns (probably of Carrara marble) across the front and along either flank.

THE FORUM OF AUGUSTUS

The Forum of Augustus rose to the north east of the Forum Romanum, perpendicular to the Forum Julium. Building operations began in 37 BC, during the time of troubles with Sextus Pompey, and were completed in 2 BC. The Temple of Mars the Avenger, which still dominates the open square, was approached by a flight of steps and was set inside a colonnade. A massive rear wall of Gabine tufa (see page 37) sealed the Forum from the ghetto behind and provided insurance against fires, which were common in the Subura district. Suetonius' account sets the new Forum in perspective:

> Augustus' reason for constructing the Forum was the increase in population and the number of lawsuits which seemed to require a third Forum; two (the Forum Romanum and Forum Julium) were no longer sufficient. The piazza was opened to the public before the Temple of Mars was finished with the provisos that public prosecutions should be staged there away from the rest and that the selection of jurors should be by lot. Augustus had promised to build a Temple of Mars during the battle of Philippi which he waged to avenge his father. Therefore he decreed that the Senate should deliberate there about war and requests for triumphal processions, that those who were leaving Rome to assume military commands should be escorted from it, and that those who returned victorious should lodge there the tokens of their triumphs. [Suetonius, *Augustus* 29]

The sculpture of the Augustan Forum was clearly intended as

propaganda: toga'd and breastplated statues, ancestors of Augustus, real and mythical, victorious generals and eminent citizens of Rome, stood in huge semicircular niches (or recesses) behind porticoes on either side of the temple. The Julio-Claudians, starting with Aeneas, occupied the northern niche; Republican celebrities, starting with Romulus, the southern one. So Augustus gave visible expression to his claim to have restored the Republic, and the 108 statues looked on to the square – like ancestral busts in the *atrium* of a Roman house. Free-standing caryatids (columns in the form of female figures), were mounted against the upper walls of the colonnades, copied from the Erechtheum in Athens. Bronze statues probably stood in the spaces between the columns of the porticoes. The new Forum offered a monumental avenue to the Forum of Caesar, and so to the Forum Romanum, from one of the most crowded sectors of the capital.

Italy

With the advent of the Pax Augusta, civic pride and security were restored throughout the Italian peninsula and grandiose public works began to materialise. Some of the monuments were no doubt products of the *nouveaux riches* who had supported Augustus, works which would beautify a home town and ensure the builders' fame; others were donated by the Princeps, sometimes as part of a colonial settlement, sometimes as outright gifts to the populace, signalising the peace and prosperity guaranteed by the Principate. The gate of Augusta Taurinorum (Turin), wall repairs at Tergeste (Trieste), public baths at Bononia (Bologna), aqueducts at Venafrum and Brixia (Brescia), were only a small part of the imperial largesse. Vitruvius' celebrated basilica and shrine at Fanum Fortunae (Fano) was yet another civic undertaking to honour the Princeps. The Augustan repair of the Via Flaminia, from Rome to Ariminum, no doubt sparked off the building project at Fano and Vitruvius' engagement shortly after 27 BC. Agrippa provided Ostia (Rome's harbour on the Tiber) with a theatre and porticoed square which are still extant.

Gaul and Spain

Gaul and Spain witnessed important settlements and reconstruction

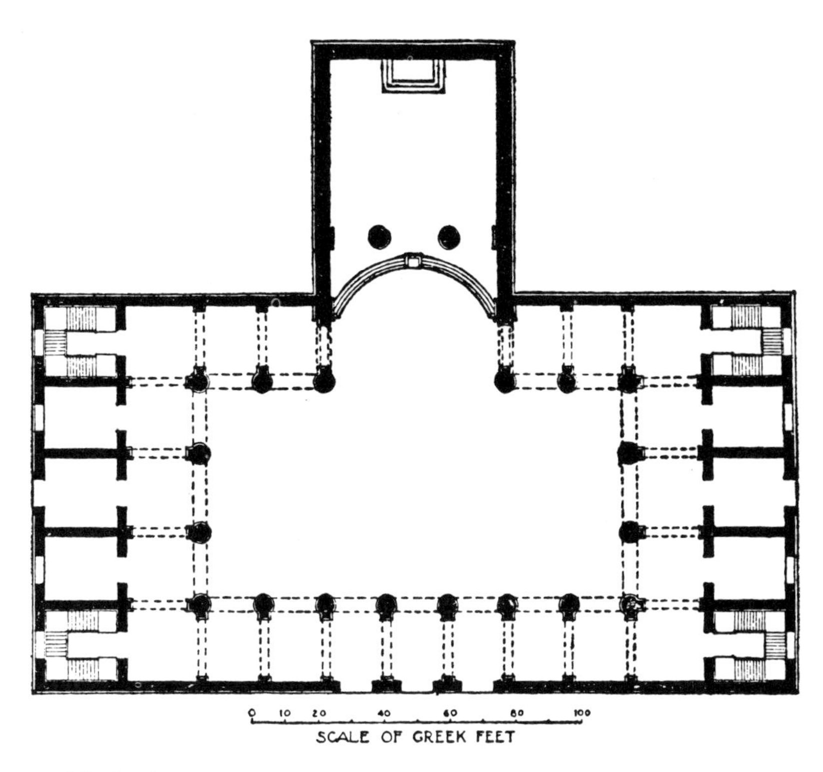

6 The Basilica of Vitruvius at Fanum Fortunae, with the Sanctuary of Augustus

programmes during the lifetimes of Vitruvius and Augustus. Caesar's victories in Gaul led to the establishment of a colony at Arelate (Arles) and of a legionary settlement at Narbo (Narbonne). L. Munatius Plancus, who restored the Temple of Saturn after his triumph, founded a colony at Lugdunum (Lyons) and at Augusta Raurica (Augst) in Switzerland. Mark Antony established a colony at Vienne, south of Lyons, and another legionary colony was settled at Arausio (Orange) in 36 BC. Forum Julii (Fréjus) was founded by Julius Caesar as a market town after the fall of Marseilles in 49 BC, but its prosperity and buildings were due to its development as a naval base after 39 BC. The artificial harbour, entirely filled in today, was provided with a lighthouse, towers at the entrance which controlled a chain boom, warehouses and arsenal, cisterns, granaries, baths, barracks and the like, for the military. Octavian sent 300 captured vessels to Forum Julii, the Toulon of Roman Gaul, after the victory at Actium (31 BC).

7 *The aqueduct at Segovia, Spain*

There are no firm dates for the extant constructions, but their remains testify to remarkable engineering skill and architectural expertise: a theatre and covered colonnade at Arles, a forum at Lyons, a Temple of Rome and Augustus at Vienne, and a marvellous theatre at Orange. The aqueduct bridge near Nîmes, the celebrated Pont du Gard, and the Maison Carrée at Nîmes, were products of Agrippan engineers and architects about 20–19 BC.

Hither and Further Spain, where pacification proved more difficult and costly for the Romans, offered additional terrain for settlement and public works. Caesar founded a veteran colony on an impressive scale at Emporiae (Ampurias); Tarragona, the capital of the Roman province of Hither Spain, boasted a Temple of Augustus (acceptable outside the confines of Italy), a Temple of Jupiter Ammon, a circus and an amphitheatre, and harbour installations. Augusta Emerita (Mérida) founded by Agrippa in 25 BC as a settlement for his veterans, adopted a square (*castrum*) plan; it was supplied with a river port, bridges, reservoir, aqueducts, walls, drains, temples, a theatre and an amphitheatre, a circus, commemorative monuments, luxury-style houses, etc. Its Guadiana River bridge, over 750 metres long and still standing, was supported by sixty arches; Agrippa's engineers supplied relieving arches and cut-water piers to reduce the pressure of floodwaters against the bridge. A reservoir, five kilometres to the north west, is a massive masonry dyke, 422 metres long, 2–3.5 metres thick and nine metres high; its capacity was 10 000 000 cubic metres of water! The aqueduct, once eleven kilometres long, is also partially extant; its piers, which support three storeys of arches, rise twenty-four metres above ground level, and are faced with granite and brick in alternate layers like the Arabic arches in the Cordoba mosque. The circus may have accommodated 30 000 spectators. The aqueduct at Segovia, which still functions, is probably Augustan; its 128 surviving arches run for nearly a kilometre and in the centre of the city stalk twenty-seven metres above the street level.

Building programmes like these were a humane contribution to the tax-paying provinces; they glorified the Princeps, his regime, and the capital; they made amends for past inhumanity and destruction; and they provided creature comforts, continuing employment, and painless romanisation.

5

The materials of construction

Structural behaviour and design

Safety requirements, ensuring his client's safety and protecting his property, are the primary responsibility of the structural engineer in any time or place. To fulfil this heavy responsibility, the engineer must fully understand the nature of his site, the uses of the structure, and the behaviour of the materials of construction. Wherever recurrent loads are expected, he must know the ability of floorings, transport surfaces (roads, bridges, etc.) and underwater structures to withstand normal and, on occasion, extraordinary pressure. The structural behaviour of the material must be thoroughly understood; a well-designed structure must be expected to carry a variety of loads without sustaining extensive damage or causing loss of life. Today the engineer is professionally and legally responsible for the satisfactory performance of his structure. Intuition and judgement based on experience are basic to the professional exercise; the decision of the experienced engineer has always been the most important factor in design.

Wood and stone

WOOD

Wood of course was the oldest and most common of Roman building materials and the expert carpentry of the Etruscans no doubt provided excellent examples. Although timber resources were neither plentiful nor nearby, wood was used for many purposes in Roman architecture and engineering: scaffolding for workmen's platforms, ladders, ramps; framework for vaulting; shuttering (against which concrete was poured), and other temporary constructions. The houses of aristocrats and monumental buildings often employed superior woods for beams and panelling.

TUFA AND TRAVERTINE

Certainly the most popular, and generally speaking, the most available and durable building material, was stone. Commonest was tufa, a mixture of pebbles, lava fragments and ashes produced by the volcanoes (long inactive) in the Alban Hills south of the Tiber, and in the hill country to the north. Tufaceous stone was a porous amalgam of varying degrees of hardness which could be easily mined and worked. Lapis Albanus (*peperino*), a blackish-grey composite, like pepper, quarried north of Lago Albano, was respected by builders for its durability and fireproof qualities and was used for heavy lintels, vaults, and column drums. Lapis Gabinus, reddish in colour, came from Gabii, twenty kilometres from Rome; its hard, fireproof nature made it a favourite. Anio tufa, a rough, brown variety, was prized for its durability, and for its low cost.

Vitruvius recognises the popularity of tufa but adds a word of caution for builders:

> Under cover (tufaceous stones) perform creditably; but in open and exposed situations, frost and mists make them crumble and disintegrate. On the sea coast too, the salt erodes and dissolves them, and they cannot withstand great heat. [2. 7. 2]

There can be no doubt that tufa was the approved material for foundations and for frame and wall construction throughout Republican times: aqueducts, theatres, temples, bridges and domestic architecture all incorporated this basic building material.

Vitruvius has a high regard for travertine, a sturdy limestone first quarried during the second century BC near Aqua Albulae (Bagni), twenty-two kilometres from Rome, on the road to Tibur (Tivoli). Like tufa, travertine, which remains popular today and is widely exported, is soft when first exposed and so makes the quarrying easy; soon afterwards it hardens. Vitruvius speaks from experience:

> Travertine and all stone of that sort can support damage whether from heavy loads, or from the elements; exposure to fire, however, it cannot endure but splits and cracks immediately. [2. 7. 2]

The travertine quarries contributed heavily to the Augustan Theatre of Marcellus and to the Flavian Amphitheatre (Colosseum). Estimates suggest that over a three-to-four-year period 200 000 tonnes of travertine were lodged in the exterior of the Colosseum and that 150–180 wagons were involved daily in transporting the sturdy material to the capital.

Brick

Sun-dried brick or adobe antedates the use of baked brick and, when combined with tufa and travertine, was the normal material for walls and facings into early Imperial times. Vitruvius has a profound respect for the antique building material and regards burnt-brick walls as very dependable.

As residential space inside the walls of Rome was extremely restricted, the citizens were forced to think in terms of vertical expansion as early as the third century BC. Vitruvius refers to established techniques of construction (but not plans) with a measure of resignation:

The present importance of the city and the population explosion have made it necessary to provide an infinite number of dwelling-units, because the ground floors could never accommodate the mass of city-dwellers. Circumstances have necessitated raising the height of buildings. Sky-scrapers, stone piers and walls of burnt brick, partitions of rubble work, and with a succession of wooden floors, provide upper storeys which offer 'penthouse' views at very great advantage. Walls are considerably elevated to accommodate a number of storeys and the Roman people have exceptional dwellings (*egregias . . . habitationes*). [2. 8. 17.]

Outside Rome, Vitruvius advocates the use of mudbrick walls with certain precautions:

Brick walls in suburban areas should be constructed as follows in order to be sound and durable. On the top of the wall lay a walling of burnt brick, about a metre in height, beneath the tiles and let it project like a coping. Then the defects customary in these walls can be avoided. For when the tiles on the roof are broken, or thrown down by the wind, so that rain-water can leak through, this burnt-brick shield will prevent the adobe from being damaged, and the cornice-like projection will deflect the drops from the vertical face, and so the walls of sun-dried brick will remain intact. [2. 8. 18.]

Prior to their use, Vitruvius recommends a two-year waiting period to allow the baked bricks to dry thoroughly. All brick walls were customarily covered with stucco. Augustus' boast, that he had found Rome adobe, but left it marble, applies largely to public buildings. Private homes and most multiple dwellings (tenement blocks and boarding houses) must have had a dreary aspect; public buildings used brick to cover the concrete core and marble or marble stucco would add the finishing touch.

Opus incertum and opus reticulatum

During Vitruvius' youth, the majority of Rome's concrete walls were covered with *opus incertum* – a style which uses tufa blocks (*tufelli*) of pyramidal shape set into the cement wall in such a way as to yield an irregular (*incertum*) design. *Opus reticulatum*, which became increasingly popular during his maturity, provided a 'network' or 'reticulate' surface pattern. The pyramidal stones were set into the concrete core with the seventy-millimetre square base exposed in a regular series. Vitruvius has pertinent remarks about both patterns of construction:

> There are two kinds of walls: *opus reticulatum*, the preference of modern times, and the antique style called *opus incertum*. Of these, the reticulate has a better appearance, but its construction makes it liable to cracks because it has beds and joints in every direction. *Opus incertum*, lying in courses with overlapping joints, produces a wall which is not beautiful but is stronger than reticulate. [2. 8. 1]

Opus incertum survives in the Porticus Aemilia in Rome, Caesar's rostra, the Sanctuary of Fortune at Praeneste (Palestrina), the amphitheatre of Pompeii, and the temple of Jupiter Anxur at Terracina. A warehouse complex (Horrea Sulpicia) behind the Porticus Aemilia, dates from about 100 BC, and is the earliest instance of the use of *opus reticulatum* in Rome. *Opus reticulatum* also appears in the substructures of Pompey's Theatre, and in the walls of Horace's villa at Licenza.

Vitruvius preferred ashlar (hewn-stone) masonry over the new departures; he had no real confidence in contemporary concrete which was still in the evolutionary stage. He was convinced that the porous tufa stone used in the rubble of concrete walls would ultimately prove unsatisfactory:

This we may learn from some tombs outside the city which are faced with marble or ashlar stone, but on the inside have masonry packed between the outer walls. Over the years the mortar loses its strength because it has been drawn out of it by the porousness of the rubble; and so the tombs collapse and disintegrate, because their joints are loosened by the settling of the binding material. [2. 8. 3]

Internal walls in lower-class housing and low-cost apartments were often constructed in *opus craticium* ('wicker-work' style), implying a wooden framework filled with rubble and mortar, plastered over with a thin stucco. Vitruvius condemns its use utterly:

As for wattle-and-daub, I could wish that it had never been invented. The more time it saves in construction and the more it gains in space, to that extent the disaster that it may cause becomes more widespread, for it is prone

8 Temple of Jupiter Anxur, Terracina, substructures

to catch fire, like torches. It seems preferable, therefore, to spend more on walls of burnt brick, than to save money with 'wattle-and-daub' and live in danger. [2. 8. 20]

Vitruvius also observes that, as with reticulate walls, so even more commonly, with walls of *opus craticium*, there is a tendency for the components to settle and so crack the wall stucco [2. 8. 20]. Experience has taught the proper approach if time and expense or multiple occupancy of a floor area are involved:

Supply a high foundation so that the partition does not come into contact with the broken stonework of the floor; for when it is lodged in this, it rots with the passage of time, then settles and falls forward, and so breaks through the surface of the plaster. [2. 8. 20]

9 Horace's Sabine Farm at Licenza

10 The House of the Lattice Work (Casa del Graticcio), Herculaneum

The House of the Lattice Work (*Casa del Graticcio*) at Herculaneum, a product of the 'sixties' AD, illustrates and justifies Vitruvius' strictures. The continued use of this style of construction is reflected in Juvenal's *Satire* 3, on city life, in the time of Trajan or Hadrian.

Marble

Our vision of Roman architecture invariably conjures up marble pavilions and palaces but in fact marble was never a prime building material. Stucco facing, scored and coloured to resemble white or polychrome marble and veneer (*crustae*), was commonly used during the first century BC. Actual marble was not easily obtained; it was costly to quarry and to transport, and the years of civil war interrupted any steady flow of luxury materials to the capital or the peninsula in general. The chief repositories of marble were the Near East and North Africa.

The influx of wealth (and the sales of proscribed properties) enabled some wealthy men to import exotic marbles for the porticoes and interiors of their mansions in order to reproduce elements of Hellenistic palaces and mansions overseas. Mamurra, Caesar's chief engineer, was the first to cover the walls of his house with marble. Sulla and Caesar, when they reconstructed elements of the Roman Forum, made abundant use of the new material. Sulla, who sacked Athens in 88 BC, brought Corinthian columns to Rome from the Temple of Olympian Zeus and used them in the refurbishing of the Temple of the Capitoline Triad. Caesar favoured the same material in his new Forum. Multi-coloured marbles gradually became a household aspiration; the later houses in Pompeii and Herculaneum and the villas at Stabiae often reflect the splendid marble peristyles, porches and flooring of early Imperial mansions. When Cicero designed a shrine for his deceased daughter Tullia, he asked Apella, a native of Chios, then resident in Rome, to assist him with the importing of Chian marble columns [*Ad Atticus* 12. 19. 1].

Horace inveighed against the exhibitionist tendencies and the luxurious displays of his age:

No ivory or gilded panelling shines in my home; no beams of Hymettian marble rest on columns quarried in remotest Africa; no heir of Attalus, I have not become absent-mindedly the owner of a palace, and no aristocratic women trail robes of Laconian scarlet for my benefit. But I do have loyalty, and a kindly vein of genius, and the man of means cultivates me, though I am poor. [1–11] At the edge of the grave you contract for the cutting of marble slabs and, forgetting the tomb, you raise a mansion, eager to extend the coastline where the sea thunders at Baiae, not wealthy enough with your mainland shore. [17–22] [Horace, *Odes* 2. 18]

Augustus' house on the Palatine, a combination of an earlier town house, once the property of Quintus Hortensius Hortalus, and of a specially constructed dwelling, a gift of the Senate, was noteworthy by reason of its rejection of marble furnishings and columns [Suetonius, *Augustus* 72].

The most accessible and certainly the most popular marble came from the quarries at Luni (Carrara). Strabo contributes a contemporary account of the Carrara quarries which were opened up by Caesar:

The quarries of both white and mottled bluish-grey marble are so numerous, and of such high quality (for they produce both monolithic slabs and columns), that the material for most of the finest art works in Rome, and elsewhere, comes from there; the marble is easily exported, because the quarries lie above the sea and the shoreline, and because the Tiber can transport the cargo from the sea up to Rome. [Strabo, 5. 2. 5]

A reception area for the incoming supplies of marble for public and private buildings was constructed along the Tiber shore of the Campus Martius near the later Hadrianic bridge, the Pons Aelia. The Augustan wharf, in the shape of a raised causeway, thirteen metres wide, projected twenty-four metres into the river. Concrete landings on either side of the causeway received the marble blocks which were removed from the barges on rollers, then lifted by enormous cranes from the landings to the top of the causeway for delivery elsewhere. Juvenal's account of congestion and perils in Rome's streets from construction wagons loaded with timber and marble (for Trajan's Forum?) must reflect earlier conditions too [*Satires* 3. 254 ff.]. Vitruvius was more familiar with tufa as building material than

11 The Sanctuary of Fortune at Praeneste (Palestrina)

marble; almost every building of note, including the Sanctuary of Fortune at Praeneste (Palestrina), the Hercules sanctuary at Tibur, the Doric Temple at Cori, and the Tabularium of Rome, was built of material from local tufa quarries, then covered with stucco and painted. However conservative, even reactionary, Vitruvius may sometimes appear, he seems to be sympathetic to the new use of marble in public buildings when he refers to the Honos and Virtus Temple of Gaius Mucius:

> If his temple had been of marble, so that in addition to its refinements it gained the prestige that comes from magnificence and costly outlay, it would rank among the foremost and greatest of buildings. [7. Pref. 17]

Rome's building programme was meant to recall the marble monuments of Periclean Athens and Attalid Pergamum: Pollio's library (Atrium Libertatis), behind Caesar's Forum, was marble; so too were the reconstructed Regia, and the glorious Temple of Apollo on the Palatine (28 BC), Octavian's own project, a victory offering for Actium. Marble was the visible sign of Rome's new *auctoritas*. But Vitruvius was not entirely enthralled. He expressed concern about the large distances between columns in the new Temple of Palatine Apollo, which might cause the architrave beams to crack [3. 3. 4]. So too, in temples of the time-honoured Tuscan style, he advocates the use of wooden beams on top of the columns [3. 3. 5]. He seems to have accepted the use of marble in theatres [5. 6. 7] although he questioned the acoustic properties of the new stone buildings like the Theatre of Pompey and the Theatre of Marcellus (still under construction), as compared with those of the older wooden theatres [5. 5. 7].

Concrete, mortar, and pozzolana

Vitruvius is characteristically guarded in his comments on the use of concrete although scholars are convinced that it was the most significant and influential of the Roman discoveries of the second century BC. The use of concrete enabled the Romans to advance far beyond their Etruscan and Greek masters. Concrete enabled the Roman engineer and architect to escape the heavy and monotonous rules of convention: curvilinear forms were a consequence. The new material, *opus caementicium*, which we call Roman concrete, was

12 *The circular marble temple of Hercules Victor, the rectangular Temple of Portunus, and Pons Aemilius*

actually a very tough mortar and was always used with a facing of some other material. The most splendid instance of its early use in Rome is the Porticus Aemilia (193 or 174 BC) whose barrel-vaulted chambers, a series of two hundred of them in rows, covered an area 320 metres long and sixty metres wide! This vast building served as a warehouse and market hall on the east bank of the Tiber. The storage chambers with their arched doors and windows, measured eight by fourteen metres and rose to a height of thirteen metres. The unknown architect was a genius of modernity. Concrete also survives in the massive podia (platform bases) of the Temple of Concord (121 BC) and in the Castor and Pollux Temple (117 BC) in the Roman Forum. To give concrete structural body, the Romans used various materials: selce (flint), tufa, pumice, broken brick and tile, and stone. Vitruvius had certainly learnt to accept the use of concrete in temple foundations [3. 4. 1] and as the basic material for high-rise flats in the capital [2. 8. 16].

The Romans discovered an excellent adhesive building material during the second century. The material was called *pulvis Puteolanus* (modern pozzolana) because quantities of it were found near Puteoli (Pozzuoli). When lime, quartz, sand and water were combined with pozzolana dust, the mortared mass became a consistent and coherent concrete which could be poured over a rubble aggregate of stone chips and brick particles, or pumice. Vitruvius seems to have had first-hand experience with pozzolana:

> There is a kind of dust which by nature causes marvellous results. It is found in the vicinity of Baiae and in the property of municipalities around Vesuvius. When this material is mixed with lime and rubble, it strengthens buildings generally, and when piers are constructed in the sea, they set hard under water. [2. 6. 1]

Vitruvius' allusion to the hydraulic properties of pozzolana accords with the study of harbour and seaside villa sites along the shores of Campania, Tuscany and Latium. The material most commonly used for aggregate in the hydraulic concrete was a soft volcanic tufa, often of a yellow-brown variety (*tufo giallo*). The Augustan breakwater pier (now submerged) at Puteoli, the naval installations at Cumae and Misenum, and the Portus Julius at Lake Avernus, used this local material with great success. Baian pozzolana was used extensively throughout Italy until the mid-first century AD when fresh sources and new ingredients were discovered.

Concrete was used commonly during Vitruvius' lifetime. Poured or stamped into wooden frames or moulds, it served for conduit pipes, parts of aqueducts, harbourworks, public and private, and, most impressively, for soaring vaults, arches, and apses.

Vaults and domes

There are two simple forms suited to carrying forces by compression alone – the column and the arch. The characteristic forms of building in Greek and Roman society accommodated to the column, thereby providing a trabeated (post and beam) architecture. Unlike the column, the arch form is designed to distribute the point load to foundation points, i.e. to support a weight at the centre of an open span of length between two points. All arch forms exert large outward horizontal forces (or thrusts) at their bases and in single-span arches these forces must be resisted by supporting foundations.

The arch as an incorporated structure and as a visible element had been used both by the Etruscans and the Greeks of South Italy before Rome adopted the form for bridges, barrel vaults and arcades. The recently excavated Porta Rosa at Velia, south of Paestum, is a double-arched gateway in a wall system dating from the fifth century BC. Tunnel and groined vaults and domes are merely extensions of the characteristic model, the arch. The Tabularium (Rome's archive building) has a long tunnel vault.

Man-made shells of reinforced concrete can be commonly seen in our contemporary architecture in auditoria, arenas, airline terminals, stores, even churches. Water and fuel storage tanks are other instances of shells stressed primarily in tension. The high efficiency, enlarged accommodation, and pleasing lines of a well-designed shell, or domed structure make it an attractive form.

The Romans were quick to develop the form after experiments with concrete had shown its essential fitness. Conical vaults, with flat sides, appear in cold-water plunge pools after the Stabian Baths at Pompeii. Vitruvius' accounts of vaultings for bath buildings imply the use of concrete and a wooden frame, but neither account agrees with vaulted forms which derive from the late Republic [5. 10. 3; 7. 3. 3]. The grandiose bath building at Baiae ('Temple of Mercury'), contemporary with Vitruvius, shows that wooden forms and poured concrete were used on a scale far exceeding the Vitruvian instances.

13 The domical Bath of Mercury, Baiae

But his emphasis on reinforcement, consisting of either a wooden or metal skeleton, with a web of concrete, tiles, or reeds, is always characteristic of Roman vaulting. Roman architects, into late Imperial times, continued to reinforce their concrete with built-in ribs.

The vaulted style proliferated and structures became increasingly 'rhetorical' and monumental. The stupendous dome of the Hadrianic Pantheon, the vaults and domed rooms of the Imperial Baths of Diocletian and of the Basilica of Constantine, symbolise imperial authority; they proclaim a message of balance and order in brick and concrete.

6

Men and machines

The tools of the profession

The basic 'tools' of the stonemason and bricklayer differed little from their modern counterparts: brush, calipers, rake, and trowel. Surveying, refined by the Etruscans and Greeks, was essential to every sort of building or planning exercise. The Etruscan surveyor's table (*groma*), plummet, surveyor's stakes, and set square were readily available. Vitruvius describes the *chorobates*, an improved version of the earlier surveyor's table:

> The *chorobates* is a straight plank about six metres long. At the extremities it has legs, made exactly alike and attached at right angles to the extremities of the straight-edge, and also cross-pieces, fastened by tenons, which connect the straight-edge and the legs. These cross-pieces have vertical lines drawn upon them, and plummets hang from the plank over each of the lines. When the plank is in position, and the plumb-lines strike both lines alike and at the same time, they indicate that the instrument stands level. [8. 5. 1]

The *chorobates* also served as a water-level when it was fitted with a groove containing water on the upper side, one-and-a-half metres long; when the water rose uniformly to the rims of the groove, the instrument was level. To survey relatively long distances, Roman engineers employed the *diopter*, a water-level, fixed on a tripod stand, with vertical and horizontal movements and cross-line sights. The instrument was used with a graduated levelling-staff which moved a large sighting-disc, so that readings were taken at the staff itself for want of telescopic sights. It has been called 'perhaps the most ingenious instrument that the ancient world produced'. Together, these instruments enabled the Roman engineer to determine horizontal direction, to erect houses, lay roads, and build aqueducts.

MEASURED DRAWINGS AND GRAPHIC DEVICES

Only a modest number of plans in mosaic and marble are extant. The best clue to Roman draughtsmanship is the enormous Forma Urbis Romae (c. AD 200), a partly-preserved plan of Rome inscribed on marble and originally exhibited on the walls of Vespasian's Forum of Peace. Drawings and completed buildings suggest that the major measurements of Roman buildings were usually multiples of five Roman feet. The impressive road-cutting at Tarracina (Latium) by the sea, the work of Trajan's engineers, is marked and numbered in three-metre vertical intervals to a total height of 110 Roman feet.

THE MACHINES

All of the aids to the construction process were available to Vitruvius and his colleagues: ladder, cog wheel and lever, block and pulley, windlass, wagon, cribs, and shutterings, frames, etc. Large-scale buildings required the crane for unloading, hoisting, and positioning of the larger stone members. A relief from the tomb of the Haterii shows a crane during building operations, with treadwheel power.

The labour force

By all accounts, the architect-engineer might be a free citizen, freedman, or slave. Technically, he was the master-craftsman. The constructions of the Augustan age were products of both semi-skilled and unskilled labour. Master-craftsmen (carpenters, stonecutters, pavers etc.) were undoubtedly available; but the movement of materials, the mixing and carrying of mortar, the laying of aggregate or movement of materials, with proper direction, required more muscle than skill. Location, circumstances, and finance determined whether the work could be performed by slaves, soldiers, or prisoners. The water-supply required vast gangs of workers, mostly slaves. Provincial monuments and engineering projects tended to be products of the military, the local citizens, or specially-hired gangs of workmen.

GUILDS

Master-craftsmen during Republican times often formed associations

14 Crane with treadmill, used in building operations

or *collegia* in order to share ideas, discuss policies, and swap experiences. Marble-workers, stone-dressers, inscription-cutters, sculptors, and pavers are numbered among the Republican guilds;

15 Mosaic, showing builders and an architect

they provided a measure of social life, dinners and entertainment, and often assisted with the burials of their members.

7
Town-planning

The mistakes of the past

Despite new construction in the Forum Romanum, the new Fora of Caesar and Augustus, and urban renewal measures in the Campus Martius, there was no means of concealing Rome's traffic and housing problems. The main causes were unplanned growth and unsystematic building. Livy's contemporary comment (c. 27 BC) reveals the unplanned horror of the capital:

Sewers originally laid down in public ground now run everywhere beneath private houses; it is like a city that has been created by squatting rather than properly proportioned. [Livy, 5. 55]

But the mistakes of the capital were not repeated in the provincial towns. Pompeii, Herculaneum, Cosa, Paestum, and Ostia are instances of rational and careful planning during Republican times. The fact that some of these towns were earlier Greek settlements unquestionably influenced their plans and construction.

Decor and the city-scape

Vitruvius' remarks on the ideal proportions of the forum and the appropriate location for temples and public buildings are based on a rational theory of appropriateness (the *decor*-theory). When applied to architecture and town-planning, this theory required architects and draughtsmen to determine whether the form of a building was appropriate to its function and location and whether the details of the building were appropriate to its total form:

The size of a forum should be adjusted to population figures, so that it may not be too cramped for use nor resemble a wasteland through a lack of people. To determine its breadth, divide the length into three parts, with two assigned to the breadth. Its plan will be oblong, and its ground plan adaptable for performances. [5. 1. 2]

Like some modern champions of environmental reform, Vitruvius cautions against careless city-planning and housing projects:

After the town has been walled, the next procedure is the allocation of building sites inside the wall, and the laying out of streets and alleys with regard to climatic conditions. They will be properly laid out if precautions are taken to exclude winds from the alleys. Chilly winds are unpleasant, hot winds enervating, and moist winds noxious. [1. 6. 1]

The sites for sanctuaries are to follow rules and practice often visible in the Hellenistic cities of Asia Minor and Magna Graecia (southern Italy and Sicily) in Vitruvius' time and our own:

If the walls are by the sea, ground close to the harbour should be chosen as the site for the forum but if inland, in the centre of the town. The temples (of tutelary deities and) of Jupiter, Juno, and Minerva should occupy the highest ground with a view of the largest possible sector of the ramparts; Mercury (god of trade) should be in the forum, or, like Isis and Serapis, in the business quarter; Apollo and Father Bacchus near the theatre; Hercules at the circus in communities which lack gymnasia and amphitheatres; Mars outside the walls but at the training ground, and also Venus, but near the harbour . . . (Vulcan) and Ceres should also be planted outside the city.
[1. 7. 1–2]

The decor-theory suggests that the architectural order of the temple should be appropriate to the deity worshipped in it: Doric, for martial deities like Minerva, Mars, and Hercules; Corinthian for softer, flowery deities like Venus, Flora, and the nymphs; and Ionic, midway between Doric austerity and Corinthian softness, for deities of 'hybrid' nature like Juno, Diana, and Bacchus.

Pompeii, Herculaneum, Ostia, Paestum, and Cosa as town-plans and operational communities reflect much of the wisdom and experience inherited by Vitruvius. Colonial foundations and veteran settlements, at home and abroad, commonly show remarkable foresight and resource on the part of their anonymous planners. There is usually a practicality of arrangement within the town walls: markets are restricted to serviceable areas; porticoes provide meeting-places; covered halls (basilicas) suitable for legal and commercial business are extensions of the civic centre.

8

Hydraulic engineering

Water is best

Planning and sanitation were closely linked in the practical Roman mind. Roman cities made prodigal use of water for baths, fountains, pools, and the household needs of the populace. Sanitary engineering provided drains, sewers, and public latrines. Strabo comments enthusiastically on Roman engineering skill as evidenced in the capital:

The Romans showed the greatest foresight in matters which the Greeks tended to discount as unimportant, such as road construction, aqueducts, and sewers to carry the filth of the city into the Tiber. ... The sewers, vaulted, with closefitting stones, have sometimes room enough for loaded hay wagons to pass through them. Water is conducted into the city by aqueducts in such quantities that veritable rivers flow through the city and the sewers; almost every residence has cisterns and service-pipes and copious fountains – the prime concern of Marcus Agrippa, although he also beautified the city with many other structures. [Strabo, 5. 3. 8]

DRAINAGE SYSTEMS

Rome's drains (and aqueducts) owed much to Etruscan experience and tradition. Etruscan drainage canals, for agricultural use, are found repeatedly in the nearby territory of Veii. They are excavated out of the soft tufa rock of the vicinity. Similar devices appear in the towns. The excavations at Marzabotto (near Bologna) and at Veii show careful provision for street drainage by means of subterranean channels (*cuniculi*) and open conduits.

The celebrated Cloaca Maxima (Great Drain) of Rome was built, according to the tradition, by Tarquinius Priscus, the Etruscan King of Rome. The original drain was probably an open conduit designed to serve the needs of the Forum. The Republican remains show a flooring of polygonal lava stones and walls of tufa blocks, sometimes three to five layers deep; travertine also appears in some sectors. The covered drain received a barrel-type vaulting of wedge-shaped stones seven to nine layers thick, but only three layers thick at the Tiber bank. Sometimes the drain was simply covered by stone slabs like an aqueduct channel.

Vitruvius as water-man

Vitruvius is most informative on methods of locating water, where to look, tests to determine good water from bad, and above all, methods of conveying water. Much of his wisdom probably derives from Hellenistic science as well as from personal experience. Three methods of conveying water are examined: masonry channels, lead pipes, and earthenware conduits. His account of masonry channels is detailed and enlightening:

Let the structural masonry be as solid as possible, and let the bed of the channel (*specus*) have a gradient of not less than six millimetres every thirty metres and let the masonry structure be arched over, so that the water may be protected from the sun. When it has reached the city walls, build a reservoir (*castellum*) with a distribution tank in three compartments, joined with the reservoir to receive the water, and let the reservoir have three pipes, one for each of the connecting tanks, so that when the water overflows from the two outside tanks, it may deliver into the middle one. [8. 6. 1]

The central reservoir was designed to service different areas:

From this central tank, pipes will be laid to all the basins and fountains; from the second tank, to the baths, so that they may furnish an annual revenue for the state; and from the third, to private houses, so that the water supplied for public use will not run short; for private persons will be unable to divert it if they have only their own limited supply from headquarters. That is the reason why I have made these divisions; individuals who take a private supply into their houses may, by their water taxes, help to maintain the conducting of the water by the contractors. [8. 6. 2]

The third outlet can also be turned off in time of drought so as not to diminish the public supply.

The course of the aqueduct, which must maintain a constant gradient within the channel, may require tunnels:

If there are hills between the city and the source of supply, underground channels must be dug, and brought to a level at the gradient mentioned earlier. If the earthbed is tufa or stone, the channel may be cut in it; but if it is of earth or sand, vaulted masonry walls must be constructed for the water channel with shafts (for inspection and cleaning) provided every thirty-six metres. [8. 6. 3]

Surface exploration today frequently reveals mounds of lime deposit removed by the troops or slave maintenance crews along the line of vanished aqueducts.

Vitruvius recommends a gradient of not less than six millimetres to every thirty metres of aqueduct. Arches, single-tier, double or even triple, were used to cross steep valleys. The inverted siphon, invoked when valleys were particularly steep, was based on the principle that water seeks its own level. The siphon effect forced water to flow uphill after it had descended from a higher place.

Lead pipes were the normal conduits for water from city aqueducts to public fountains. The lead was imported from Spain and Sardinia in Augustan times. The metal was cast into flat sheets on a stone form with the name of the public official in charge of water supply incised or stamped on the metallic surface. The flat sheet was then bent, soldered, and given the required fitting. Lead pipes, frequently evident in Pompeii and Herculaneum, were the normal channels for water from public reservoirs into private dwellings; these pipes were often stamped with the name of the house-owner to help identify pipes which required repairs and also to prevent fraudulent use of piping.

If the water is to be supplied in lead pipes, first a reservoir (*castellum*) must be built at the source; then pipes, with an interior area corresponding to the amount of water, are to be chosen; these pipes are to be laid from this reservoir to the reservoir inside the city walls. The pipes should be cast in lengths of at least three metres. When a pipe is made from a plate fifty digits in width, it will be called 'fifty' (*quinarius*) and so on with the rest. [8. 6. 4]

The lead pipes could cross small depressions on substructures or circumvent the larger; but if the depression were a continuous valley, the pipes would descend into the valley and cross its floor on substructures. When they reached the upward slopes on the opposite side, the water in the pipes expanded somewhat and mounted the slope. A horizontal stretch (*venter*) had to be provided across the valley floor to prevent the water pressure from bursting the pipe [8. 6. 5–6]. Small valves along the length also helped relieve the air pressure in the pipes [8. 6. 6]. Reservoirs might be planted at intervals of about eight kilometres, but never in the depressions, only on the lines of the continuous overall slopes. They served to limit the effect of breakages in the pipe lines and assisted repairs.

Clay piping was the most economical form of conduit. The walls of the pipe were to be no less than two fingers thick, and each section of pipe required a tongue at one end to permit tight fits. The joints were to be caulked by a mixture of quicklime and oil [8. 6. 8]. If extra pressure were anticipated the joints had to be sealed in a hole pierced through a standing block of Gabine stone (see page 37). A final precaution is added:

Ashes are to be put in first, so that if any of the joints have not been sufficiently coated, they may be coated (and sealed) with ashes. [8. 6. 9]

Vitruvius points out several advantages of using clay pipes rather than masonry conduits and lead pipes:

Earthenware water pipes have the following advantages. First, during construction, if a fault is discovered, anybody can repair the damage. Secondly, water from clay pipes is much more wholesome than water from lead pipes; lead is known to be harmful because white lead is derived from it, and this is said to be injurious to the human system. Plumbers offer an instance of this since in them the natural body complexion is affected by pallor.... Hence, water should not be conducted in lead pipes, if we want to have it wholesome. That the taste is better when it comes from clay pipes may be demonstrated by everyday living practices, for although our tables are piled high with silver vessels, everybody uses earthenware to retain purity of taste. [8. 6. 10–11]

Strabo's praise of Roman hydraulic engineering must have matched the appreciation of the Roman populace. Scholars have estimated that the net result of the new water works from 33 BC onwards was perhaps to augment the water supply by about seventy-five per cent. By the third century AD, eleven major aqueducts brought water into the capital from distances of up to ninety kilometres. The Nîmes aqueduct, the Pont du Gard, is part of one which ran for fifty kilometres from a spring at Uzès; it provided every town dweller with 450 litres per day. The huge uncemented masonry piers and arches which stalk across the Campagna today, between the Fiumicino airport and Rome, still excite admiration.

Reservoirs and cisterns

A cistern, fed by the rain water from the catch-basin (*impluvium*) in the *atrium*, was the normal complement of any Republican dwelling-place whether town-house or villa. Before the advent of a sophisticated water-supply the cistern was the principal source of water for household uses. After the hole is dug out, Vitruvius prescribes that the walls and floors of the cistern be stamped or pounded hard before being lined with *opus signinum*, a waterproof cement containing crushed terracotta chips. Cisterns should properly contain two or three compartments to allow for settling or purification:

> Water will become more limpid, and retain its taste without any smell, if the mud has somewhere to settle; otherwise it will be necessary to clear it by adding salt. [8. 6. 15]

Household cisterns normally fell into disuse after the city was able to provide water directly to houses by lead or clay conduits, although baths within the house might continue to draw on cistern water delivered via town aqueducts.

The largest cisterns in Italy are found on Imperial estates (e.g. Tiberius' Villa Jovis at Capri, and Domitian's Villa at Albanum), and in the neighbourhood of the naval base at Misenum. Most awesome is the Piscina Mirabilis ('Marvellous Pool') excavated in a tufa hill at Bacoli, near Baiae. The dimensions are impressive: seventy metres long by twenty-five wide, and about fifteen metres deep. The interior contains twelve rows of huge columns along the major axis, and four rows along the minor. The columns, cruciform in design, have convex footings, and the majority carry two arches. There is a central trench or catchbasin, and light-shafts, about one metre square, appear where the columns intersect at roof level. The reticulate and brick bonding courses of the interior walls and column facing are covered with *opus signinum*. This enormous freshwater cistern, product of

16 The Piscina Mirabilis (cistern), Bauli (modern Bacoli)

Agrippa's engineers during the 30s or 20s BC, was designed to store fresh water for the populous bayside holiday area, and for the naval station at nearby Misenum. The catchbasin and lightshafts no doubt assisted the purification of the water provided by seasonal rains and by the Aqua Serino, the Augustan aqueduct. The capacity of the tank was 12 600 cubic metres. Wells were also lined with hydraulic cement (*opus signinum*). A stone curb (*puteal*) normally ringed the well opening of household cisterns. Sometimes upright members would frame the mouth of the well and support a horizontal beam with slots for the axle of a pulley. Household wells and cisterns might also serve as refrigerators for wines and perishables.

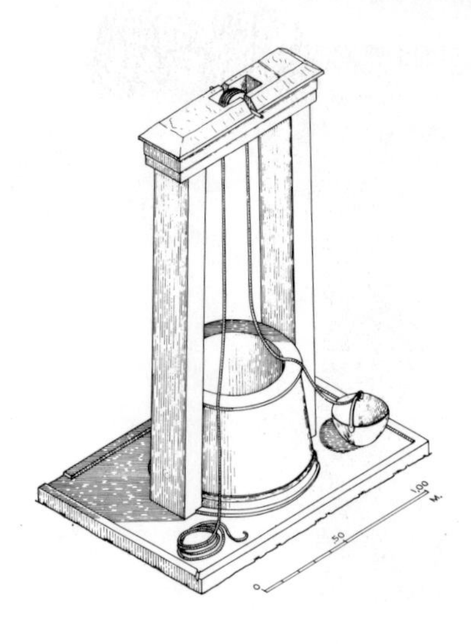

17 Wellhead and windlass

Waterways and canals

Caesar's scheme to canalise the Tiber to provide more rapid river transit and to safeguard the city against floods was thwarted by his assassination. Probably the most celebrated canal in Italy ran through the Pomptine Marshes, south-east of Rome. Although the Appian Highway ran through the marshy area, travellers who sought to escape the menace of highwaymen and the discomfort of carriage or horseback through the dreary flatlands, chose the parallel barge-canal. Horace describes a nightmarish passage through the marshes as a member of a diplomatic party bound to reconcile differences between Octavian and Antony in 37 BC [*Satires* I. 5. 9–24]. The drainage trenches were not entirely effective; the marsh remained uncultivated and largely unsettled. The Italian dictator Mussolini finally completed the drainage programme following the lines marked out by the ancient surveyors of the mid-second century BC.

Harbours

The militarisation of the ancient cult and oracular area near Cumae involved several large-scale engineering projects. To combat the menace of Sextus Pompey, the son of Pompey the Great and piratical

18 M. Vipsanius Agrippa

rival and thorn in the side of the second Triumvirate, Agrippa and Octavian undertook to revitalise the old Greek harbour at the foot of the Cumaean acropolis, and to design a new harbour, Portus Julius, near Puteoli. The Portus Cumanus, recently discovered, is an enlarged version of the Greek harbour which had silted up over the centuries. To combat the old problem, the Roman engineers built a canal from Torregaveta, a nearby headland, to Lacus Acherusius (modern Lago Fusaro), and from that shallow lake to the Portus Cumanus. Seawater introduced into the channel at Torregaveta continued into Lago Fusaro; the lower elevation of the Portus enabled the water to proceed, under pressure, from the lake into the harbour and so out to sea. So the overflow channel provided scouring water for the harbour and kept it free of sand.

The Portus Julius, eulogised by Vergil (*Georgics* 2. 180–184), is usually ascribed to Agrippa's architect-engineer, L. Cocceius Auctus. Lake Avernus, the reputed entrance to Hades, was converted into a major naval basin and construction centre. A canal was dug to connect Avernus with the shallower waters of Lake Lucrinus which lay along the shoreline of the bay of Puteoli. A natural causeway, called the Via Herculea (Hercules' Highway), which separated Lake Lucrinus from the bay, was breached in two places to provide access for ships to the outer and thence to the inner basin. Today the Via Herculea lies underwater, but divers have detected the masonry

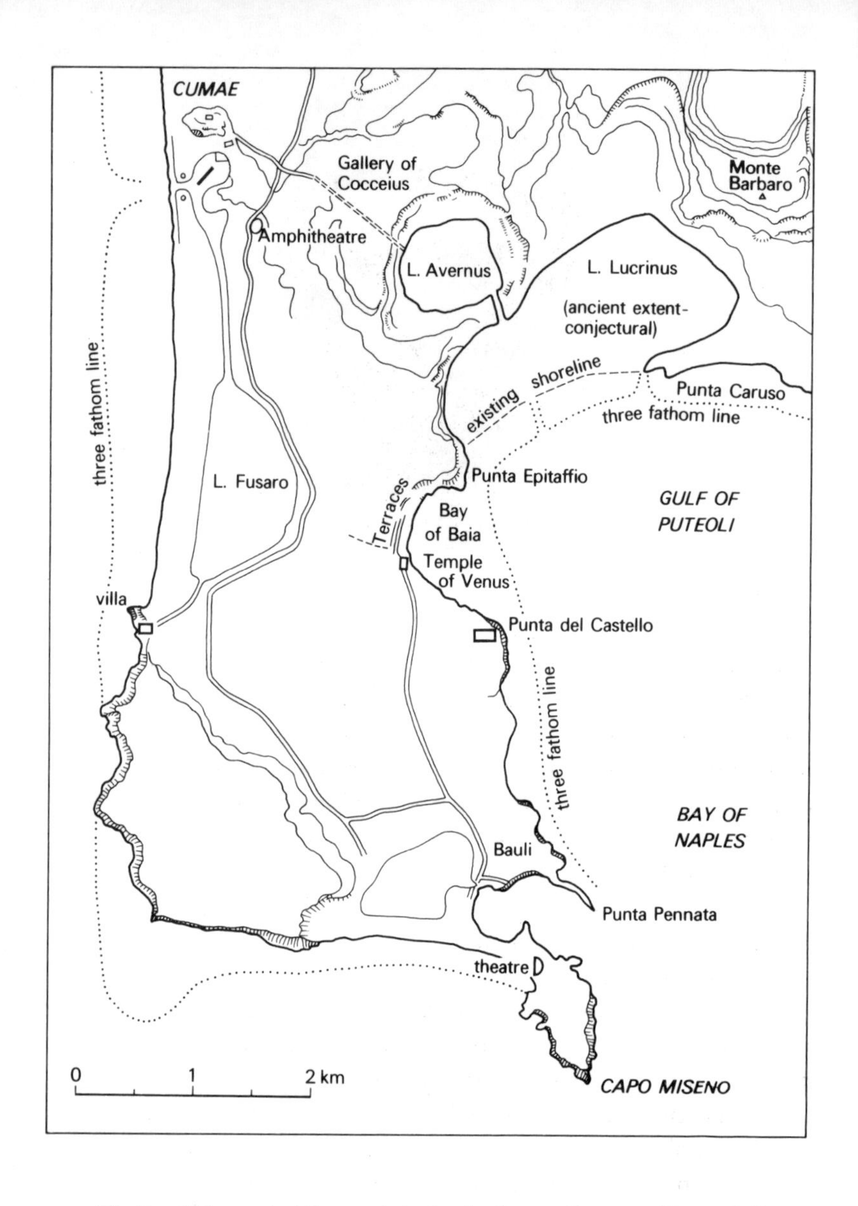

19 The Bacoli Peninsula (Campania), showing Portus Cumanus, Portus Julius, and the naval base at Cape Misenum

blocks which once lined the breakwater and made it a practicable artery for traffic between Puteoli and the Baian shore. The harbour entries were crossed by lift bridges. The canal which linked the two lakes was aligned with the western gap (towards Baiae) in the causeway. The canal, nearly 400 metres long, the modernised harbour facility at Cumae, and the new Portus Julius, are token of resolute defensive measures taken against Sextus Pompeius between 38 and 37 BC.

BREAKWATERS AND MOLES

Vitruvius offers practical advice on the technical aspects of constructing breakwaters, no doubt reflecting Roman experience with commercial harbour installations at Puteoli (Pozzuoli), and with the naval installations at Portus Cumanus and Portus Julius. The local hydraulic cement possessed ideal properties for the great underwater piers which protected the larger harbours and port installations and supported the jetties and seaside porticoes of Italian villas. A small mural, retrieved from Stabiae, probably depicts the harbour of Puteoli, with colonnaded street, market buildings, jetties and piers.

20 *Waterfront mural (Puteoli?), from Stabiae*

In a place carefully determined, cofferdams (watertight structures) with their sides formed of oak stakes with ties between them, are to be driven down into the water and firmly fixed there; then the lower surface inside, under water, must be levelled and dredged, using a working platform of beams laid across; and finally, concrete from the mortar trough . . . must be heaped up until the empty space inside the cofferdams has been filled by the wall.

[5. 12. 3]

Where currents or the open sea made underwater work impossible, concrete blocks had to be constructed on the seashore and, with nature's assistance, could be toppled into the sea. Vergil, a Campanian resident, uses a constructional simile [*Aeneid* 9. 710–716] when he compares the fall of a warrior to that of a prefabricated construction block into the off-shore waters of Baiae.

HARBOUR INSTALLATIONS

Vitruvius, perhaps through his association with Julius Caesar and Octavian, perhaps through seeing (or participating in the construction of) the new military harbours at Cumae and the Portus Julius, offers valuable testimony on harbour installations:

Around harbours, colonnades or shipyards must be constructed, or passages from the colonnades to the business sections, and towers must be set up on either side, from which chains can be drawn across by machinery [5. 12. 1]. The general rule for shipyards will be to build them facing the north. Southern exposures, because of heat, generate rot, woodworms and shipworms and all sorts of other destructive creatures, and strengthen and nurture them. Such buildings must by no means be constructed of wood because of the hazard of fire. As for their size, no definite rule need be set, but they must be built to take the largest type of vessel, so that even if larger ships are hauled up, they may find a spacious berth. [5. 12.7]

Although Misenum certainly became the chief naval base of the Empire after Actium, there is no certainty about the exact date. After his victory at Actium (2 September, 31 BC), Octavian anchored the 300 captured warships in the harbour of Forum Julii (Fréjus) in Provence, which probably indicates that Misenum was still not regarded as properly equipped or defensible as a naval base. The deficiencies must have been rectified in a short period, however, and the Portus Julius was allowed to decline. The Imperial harbour at

Misenum, headquarters for Pliny the Elder during the eruption of Vesuvius in AD 79, resembled the earlier Portus Julius in comprising two basins. The inner lake, the so-called Mare Morto (Dead Sea), was joined by a short canal to the outer basin. The outer harbour, fourteen metres deep, ensured passage and anchorage for the largest warships and merchantmen, and the port was well protected from southerly and westerly winds. To guard against silting, tunnels were let into two confronting promontories as sluice devices. A connecting canal, spanned by a wooden bridge high enough to permit the passage of masted ships, provided access to the inner basin where the main dockyards, warehouses, arsenals, barracks and the like, were located.

Baths and heating systems

During the late Republican era Romans, both in the capital city and in country retreats, found pleasurable recreation in the ritual of bathing. Roman baths (*thermae*) catered for both the body and the mind; exercise, bathing, and massage were accompanied by discussion, gossip and reading.

Since he was interested in hydraulics, Vitruvius has something to say about bath-buildings. The sequence of procedures was common to almost every bath system which catered for private citizens, clubmen and women. Lobbies and dressing rooms (*apodyteria*) led into a succession of rooms – a tepid chamber (*tepidarium*), a super-heated baking and steaming room (*calidarium*, *sudatorium*), and a cold water plunge bath or swimming pool (*frigidarium*). Although the swimming pool might adjoin the changing-room and be used exclusively on hot days, the entire system was compact, civilised and reliable.

Vitruvius encourages the economic deployment of heat (or energy) in the civic bath complexes:

> We must ensure that the hot baths (*calidaria*) in the women's and men's wings adjoin each other, and are located in the same spot; for this will enable the same furnace (*praefurnium*) to serve both areas and their fittings. [5. 10. 1]

To conserve the heat, and to avoid draughts, door posts were often inclined so that doors left open would close automatically by their own weight.

During the first century BC, *thermae* showed great advances in utility and amenity. Through the enterprise of Gaius Sergius Orata, a speculator and land promoter on the Campanian coastline, new heating systems began to appear in the pleasure-villas and public baths of the region. Vitruvius refers to the new radiant heating system:

The hanging floors (*suspensurae*) of the hot bath rooms should be constructed as follows. First the ground surface should be paved with 400 mm tiles, sloping towards the furnace in such a way that, if a ball is thrown in, it will not be arrested inside but will return automatically to the furnace room; thus the heat will spread more easily under the floor. Pillars made of 200 mm bricks should rest on the ground at such intervals that 600 mm tiles can be placed to cover them. The pillars should be 600 mm high, laid in clay mixed with hair, and covered on top with 600 mm tiles which support the floor. [5. 10. 2]

The Vitruvian hypocaustic (under-heating) system is more elaborate than the arrangement in the Stabian and Forum Baths at Pompeii, or of the men's and women's baths at Herculaneum. But the principle is common: hot air, circulating under the floors of the steam rooms (*calidaria*) and up the walls, sometimes into the vaulted ceilings, through hollow tiles, provided a circulation system of great efficiency. Vitruvius may say little about the adaptability of the vaults to contemporary architectural forms, but he has firm ideas about steam bathrooms:

The *laconicum* ('steam room') and sweating chambers should adjoin the tepid room, and their height to the springing of the dome should be equal to their width. An aperture should be left in the middle of the dome with a bronze disc hanging from it by chains. By raising and lowering it, the temperature of the sweating bath can be regulated. The chamber itself should be circular, so that the force of the fire and heat may spread evenly from the centre around the entire circumference. [5. 10. 5]

Baths of the early (and later) Imperial period in Pompeii and Herculaneum substantiate what Vitruvius says, although the *calidaria* are normally vaulted rooms rather than circular or domed chambers.

Baiae, however, offers an important illustration of Vitruvius' prescription for domical bath construction in the so-called 'Temple of Mercury' rising below the terraced imperial abode lining the hillside and recently uncovered by Italian archaeologists. The 'temple', in reality a domical rotunda, is part of a system of constructions: a spacious *apodyterium*, a *calidarium*, large plunge pool, and lounge or rest room (*schole*). The design is spectacular. The dome rises from a robust concrete cylinder faced with *opus reticulatum*; the fabric is capped by a central ring opening (*oculus*) where the vault is only 533 mm thick. The interior diameter of the rotunda is twenty-one and a half metres and although the building is partly flooded today, the original height was probably equal to the diameter [cf. Vitruvius 5. 10. 5]. The inner walls contain two large rectangular rooms and four curved niches. Four rectangular windows are let into the haunch of the vault; these, together with the *oculus* and door jambs, arc framed in tufa blocks. The dome was built by pouring concrete in successive rings against a hemispherical dome of wood; as the concrete (available nearby) was poured, a grid of ribs was built in to strengthen the dome, with lighter materials introduced as the dome rose to its full height.

The hot springs, which were (and remain) Baiae's therapeutic asset, poured into this circular swimming pool (*natatio*) from the rectangular opening of the interior against the hillside; the rectangular space directly opposite provided for the removal of the water; the four niches probably served as sitting spaces for the bathers. Axiality and symmetry and practical engineering combine marvellously in this prototype of the Hadrianic Pantheon.

Although Vitruvius is aware of the new hypocaustic system which first emerged along the Neapolitan littoral, he provides direction for older systems also:

> Three bronze cauldrons should be set over the furnace, one for hot, another for tepid, and the third for cold water, all so disposed that the amount of water which flows out of the hot water cauldron may be replaced from that for tepid water and in the same way the cauldron for tepid water may be supplied from that for cold. The arrangement should allow the tortoises (*testudines*) for the hot basins to be heated from the same furnace. [5. 10. 1]

The Stabian Baths at Pompeii offer an admirable illustration of the Vitruvian account. The women's and men's systems both use the same furnace, and the bathing pool in the *calidarium* (which could accommodate ten persons at once) is a sunken half-cylinder (i.e. 'tortoise-shell') which rests on a special flue coming from the nearby furnace.

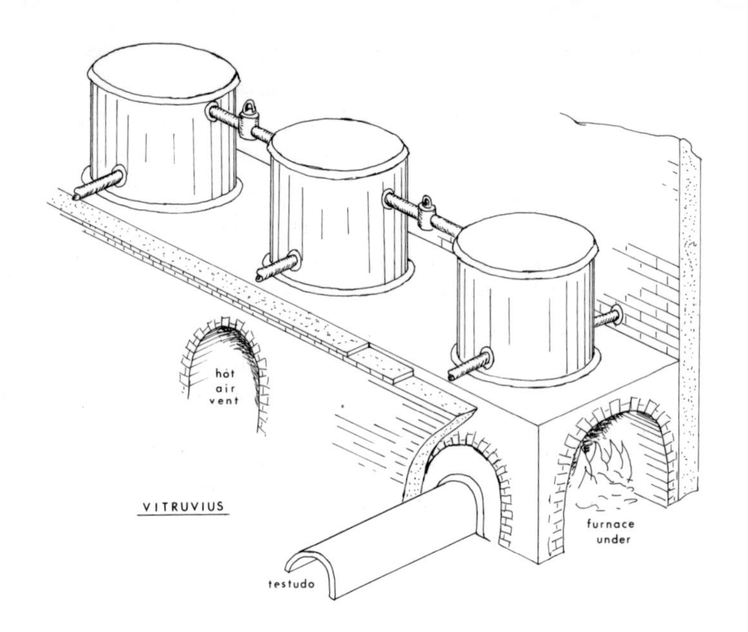

21 Heating system for baths, according to Vitruvius

Although Vitruvius indicates that baths in country houses should adjoin the kitchen (as in the Greek world), he provides no additional information about the arrangements of baths in private houses.

9

Avenues of communication

Construction of major roads

The Roman emphasis on utility in building was nowhere more strikingly reflected than in their great roads which ultimately extended to every corner of the Empire. They eventually covered a distance equal to ten times the circumference of the earth at the equator. They are an abiding symbol, in every province, of Roman energy and organising genius. These highways were the key to the unification of the Italian peninsula and of the Roman world; their role as carriers and promoters of commerce, troop movements, postal service and so on, was incalculably great.

In Roman road building, as in hydraulic engineering, the Romans began where the Etruscans left off. By the end of the fifth century BC the Etruscans had acquired a proficiency in building gravel and unpaved roads; they cut passes out of the tufa rock, with a gradient suitable for wheeled traffic, between valleys and upland plateaus. Drainage channels prevented rainwater from scouring the road surface. When the Romans first occupied parts of southern Etruria, they simply adopted the Etruscan system and were content to borrow and adapt Etruscan roadway engineering techniques. Only after 230 BC, with the introduction of paved surfaces and arched bridges, did Rome register any great engineering originality.

The earliest Roman road, the Via Appia, was built by M. Claudius Appius Caecus, censor in 312 BC. Although nearly 2300 years old, portions of it still carry traffic today. Originally gravel-surfaced, it was admired for its passage through (and sometimes around) natural obstacles, and for its course across the Pomptine Marshes. It finally linked Rome with Capua and Brundisium, the embarkation port for Greece on the Adriatic.

Normally straight as an arrow, like some modern motorway,

Roman roads are splendid examples of engineering expertise. The paving blocks were usually flint (selce), polygonal in shape, and closely fitted without benefit of mortar. Non-arterial roads were made of paving blocks laid in a trench and packed with earth and selce chips.

The major roads, often four and a half metres wide between the kerbs, required careful preliminary steps, bringing into play the surveyor's table (*groma*), and levelling table (*chorobates*). Marginal trenches were dug by gangs of labourers to the stipulated foundation depth, and the loose earth, etc., was removed. The roadbed was tampered (i.e. rammed down to consolidate it) and the foundation (*pavimentum*) of lime-mortar or sand was laid. Next came the first course (*statumen*) of fist-sized stones, cemented together with mortar or clay, from 250 to 600 mm thick; over this was laid the second course (*rudus*) of 250 to 300 mm of lime concrete with an aggregate of broken stone or pottery fragments. The third course (*nucleus*) consisted of concrete made of gravel or coarse sand mixed with hot lime, placed in layers and compacted with a roller. The thickness of the *nucleus* varied from the side (300 mm) to the crown of the road (450 mm). The top course (*summum dorsum*) consisted of polygonal blocks of selce, 150 mm or more thick, set in the soft *nucleus*. Kerbs were normally 600 mm wide and 450 mm high, and paved footpaths often ran alongside.

Conduits often ran beneath the kerb with arched outlets beside the right of way to drain the surface water. Milestones, often two-metre high pillars, marked the distance from Rome and gave the name of the person responsible for building or repairing the road. Depending on the nature of the terrain, Roman highways might also exhibit supporting walls, rock-hewn causeways, bridges, and tunnels. The engineers were prepared to cope with steep gradients before succumbing to sweeping curves or hairpin turns.

Roadway loads were comparatively light for the extravagant engineering involved. The 'ruthless thoroughness' of the Roman engineers was meant to expedite traffic and impress the user. And it did.

Augustus records in his *Res Gestae* [20. 5] that he restored the Via Flaminia from Rome to Rimini; he persuaded his generals who had earned triumphs to rebuild all the other Italian roads out of their own booty [Suet. *Aug*. 30]. The Via Flaminia was predecessor to the modern Via del Corso in Rome today. It was on the west side of the

22 *The Flaminian Highway, looking towards Mount Soracte*

Via Flaminia that the Senate set up the celebrated Altar of Augustan Peace (the Ara Pacis) between 13 and 9 BC. The road had originally been constructed by Gaius Flaminius, consul in 187 BC, and traversed the countryside of Latium, Tuscany and Umbria to the northern Adriatic.

Bridges

Roman bridge-building, an early necessity in a riverside community, progressed from wooden strut forms like the Pons Sublicius, through wooden platforms laid on stone supports, to stone versions. Best known is the Pons Fabricius, bridging the river between the island (in the Tiber) and the right bank. The materials are tufa and peperino, faced with travertine. It has two main arches and an arched opening for floodwater in the central pier. Instead of introducing a series of wide-spanned arches, the Roman engineers preferred to multiply the intermediate piers which rested on sturdy underwater supports. As with Caesar's first trestle-bridge over the Rhine (*Gallic War* 4. 16–19), the piers of the stone bridges were often designed as cut-waters to break the force of the stream in full spate.

The Pons Mulvius, or Ponte Molle today, to the north of Rome, carried the Via Flaminia across the Tiber. It has associations with Cicero's suppression of the Catilinarian conspiracy, with Nero's licentious activities, and with the victory of Constantine over Maxentius in AD 312. The extant bridge dates from 109 BC. The bridge is basically constructed of tufa (and mortar), with travertine and peperino for the facing. The spans of the arches vary from fifteen and a half to twenty-four metres.

Tunnels

Tunnels are a recurrent feature of the tufaceous hillsides around Cumae and the Bay of Naples. Strabo [5. 4. 5] notices several military and communications tunnels near Naples. One, nearly a kilometre long, connecting Cumae and the shore of Lake Avernus (Portus Julius), he assigns to L. Cocceius Auctus, freedman of Lucius Cocceius and of the architect Gaius Postumius Pollio. Another tunnel, connecting the modernised harbour beneath the Cumaean citadel with the civic centre at the other side, is still accessible. The tunnel is 180 metres long; there is a monumental vestibule at ground level (near the docks) with reticulate facing and four statue niches high up in the wall; ventilation and light wells appear along its length at roof level, and an immense cave, used as water reservoir or storage chamber, opens along the right side towards the civic centre. Both tunnels, no doubt products of Cocceius' engineering skill, were designed to serve as military passageways in the event of siege at either harbour installation, the Portus Cumanus or the Portus Julius. Relief representations of the tools used by the construction crews appear on the roof of the acropolis gallery opening into Cumae's forum: axe, pick, mallet, and wedges. Cocceius also cut the tunnel connecting Puteoli and Naples through Posillipo, the tufaceous height which separates Naples from the so-called Campi Phlegraei ('Fiery Fields') towards Cumae and Baiae. His name appears later as architect of the Temple of the Deified Augustus at Pozzuoli, a splendid Corinthian temple, faced with Carrara marble, crowning the ancient acropolis.

Cocceius' tunnel through Posillipo enabled troops, and civilians, to travel between Naples and Puteoli by a lower route, one which was far more accessible and negotiable than the earlier route which passed over the Neapolitan ridge. The dimensions were impressive: six and a half metres wide, with a maximum height of twenty-one metres along the kilometre-long passage. Light and air, as at Cumae, entered by means of vents inserted regularly along the tunnel's length. Seneca (4 BC–AD 65) passed through the tunnel on one occasion with considerable (perhaps not uncommon) discomforts; his account is charged with humour and deadly earnestness at one and the same time:

When I had to leave Baiae to return to Naples, it was easy for me to convince myself that a storm was raging so that I would not have to resort to a ship again; but the road was so muddy that I might appear to have made a sea-voyage nevertheless. On that day I had to undergo the full routine of the athletes; after the anointing, I was sprinkled with sand in the Neapolitan tunnel. No place could be longer than that prison; nothing could be dimmer than those torches which helped us, not to peer through the gloom, but simply to see the darkness. Even though the place might admit some light, the dust, which is oppressive and disagreeable even in the open, would dispel the light. What an experience it is there to have the dust roll back on itself and, because it is confined without any ventilation, blow back in the faces of the people who stirred it up. We underwent two inconveniences, at the same time, both of them diametrically opposite; we struggled with mud and with dust on the same road and on the same day. [Seneca, *Epist.* 57. 1–3]

10

Roman technology

Greek invention: Roman stagnation

Vitruvius testifies repeatedly to the engineer's concern for the best (and most economical) building materials, to the proper function of the construction, and its aesthetic character. The tools, as we have seen, were simple, but the end product was often a splendid amalgam of utility and grace. Town plans, drainage and irrigation systems, aqueducts and roads, were marvels of engineering mastery and good design.

Mechanical aids to support the engineering miracles were limited and hardly responsive to innovation. When an engineer recommended to the Emperor Vespasian that he use a labour-saving device to expedite the transportation of marble columns to the Capitoline Hill, the Emperor rejected the suggestion on the ground that he must keep the masses employed on a protracted basis so that they would not starve [Suetonius, *Vespasian* 18]. There was no incentive to improve the basic technology which the Romans had inherited from the old world of Greece and the Hellenistic kingdoms. Although there was patronage, which Vitruvius enjoyed under Caesar and Augustus, for improved artillery and siege engines, none can be evidenced for peaceful operations. No one saw the advantages of wind power to raise water until the Middle Ages; although steam power was known on a modest scale, no one diverted it to the workshops or mines, or to the conveying of cargoes. Slave labour, omnipresent but not entirely oppressive, was the common machine, and labour-saving devices, which are the preoccupation of modern inventors, were neither needed nor desired. The profit motive and increased efficiency were not paramount concerns; production might yield fresh capital to increase the work force, but the improvement of production methods was apparently rarely considered.

The crane and other devices

Rome's inherited devices were all based on gears, pulleys, the screw and the lever. The crane was basically a sheer-leg tripod; the load was raised by means of compound pulleys with the motive power provided by an enormous treadwheel.

THE PULLEY

The compound pulley was commonly used for theatrical machines (to manage the stage curtain, and the awnings of the theatre and amphitheatre), for ship's tackle, and for lifting heavy materials generally. Vitruvius [10. 2. 1–10] distinguishes between hoisting machines which work with three pulleys (*trispastos*) and with five (*pentaspastos*). He notices their application to harbour and naval services:

The mechanisms described above are suitable also for the loading and unloading of ships, some being upright, and others placed horizontally on revolving platforms. Likewise ships can be hauled ashore by means of arrangements of ropes and blocks used on the ground level, without erecting poles. [10. 2. 10]

THE WATERWHEEL

The waterwheel, as described by Vitruvius, worked on the principle of water flowing beneath the wheel, which was set vertically, and by striking the blade, the water pressure induced rotation. But there was a serious limitation to its effective functioning: it was dependent on a level flow of water in the river; in the event of flood or drought, where dams were not provided, the wheel simply would not function. The Romans used the water wheel for grinding corn, extracting oil from olives, and the like. The waterwheel drove the millstones or grinders through a gearing in which the ratio was five turns of the millstone to one turn of the waterwheel.

Water mills . . . have a toothed drum fixed into one end of the axle. This is set vertically on its edge, and turns with the wheel. Next to this larger drum there is a smaller wheel, also with teeth, but set horizontally, and this is attached (to the millstone). Thus the teeth of the drum which is fixed to the axle make the teeth of the horizontal drum move and cause the grindstones to turn. A hopper, suspended over this contrivance, supplies the mill with grain, and flour is produced by the same revolution. [10. 5. 2]

A Roman waterwheel, found in the excavation of the Athenian agora, just south of the Stoa of Attalus II, follows closely Vitruvius' general principles. The fidelity with which the Athenian architect adhered to the Vitruvian plan is remarkable; the mill-wheel was built sometime between AD 457 and 474, nearly five centuries after Vitruvius wrote.

THE WATER SCREW

Designed originally by Archimedes (c. 287–212 BC) to combat seepage in the mines, the water screw was commonly used by the Romans. An example, found in El Centenillo, a mining area of Roman Spain, provides an illustration of the Vitruvian account [10. 6. 1–4]. A wooden core, with copper lugs and rivets attached, was set into a wooden frame, 500 mm in diameter and 4.2 metres long; the outer edges of the screw shaft were attached to the inside of the longitudinal laths of the container. Vitruvius notes the furnishing of the shaft:

The ends of the shaft are covered with iron [points]. To the right and left of the screw are beams, with crosspieces fastening them together at both ends. In these crosspieces are sockets lined with iron into which pivots are inserted and so the screws are turned by a treading mill. [10. 6. 3]

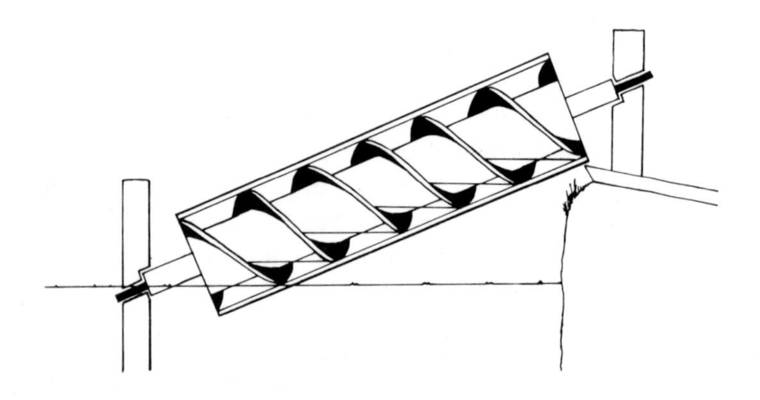

23 The 'Archimedean' screw pump for lifting water

The container (or sheath) was set on an incline of thirty to forty degrees. Each revolution of the screw would raise the water 1.8 metres vertically, then drop it into a square receptacle in which the bottom end of the next screw was inserted. Engineers have estimated that twenty screws would raise the water 30 meters. Waterwheels, set in tandem, with copper scoops set in the rims, also served to empty water from tunnels and shafts. Mine shafts might reach a depth of 200 metres; horizontal galleries often ran for 900 metres and were only about a metre high.

Spring mechanisms: scorpio and ballista

The spring was common Roman practice in bows, traps, and ballistic devices. Elasticity was the essential property, and tension was usually produced by twisting a cable composed of several strands; tension could be increased by means of levers and winches. The cables, generally speaking, were either hemp or flax products, sometimes animals' sinew, horsehair or even women's hair. The strands were tightened as much as possible before installation. Vitruvius, an arms expert, expands on the construction of the *scorpio* and the *ballista* [10. 10. 1–6]. The *scorpio* was so called because the slinging arm curved upwards like the hooked tail of the scorpion. The two-armed *ballista* could shoot either arrows or stones according to the weight of the engine; it was furnished with devices for sighting, altering elevation, and traversing. The accuracy of the aim appears repeatedly in Roman military annals and despatches like those of Julius Caesar.

BALLISTA

The *ballista*, which was convex in front, had a square frame with sidepieces. Near the ends of the crosspieces were holes through which strands of gut or horsehair passed. These were tightly wound, usually in ten layers, around nuts at both the top and bottom of the frame, and were made taut by means of a windlass. Two wooden bars passed through the middle of the bundled strands to serve as the arms of the crossbow which were moved by the torsion of the string. Their ends were connected by the bowstring which discharged the arrow, placed in a projector running in a groove. The projector was drawn back as

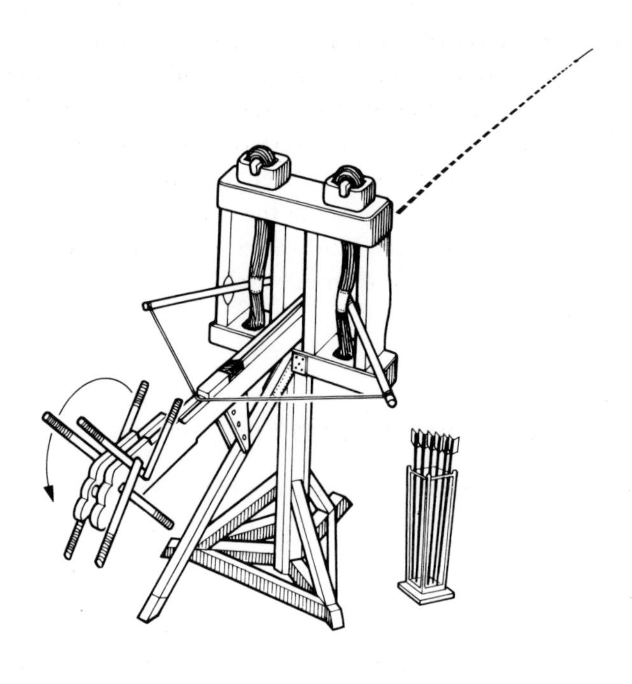

24 Ballista ('stone-thrower') adapted for arrows

far as possible by a rope worked by a windlass, and fixed in position by a catch fitting into a series of teeth. The hook (or 'hand') which held the bowstring was at the end of the projector; as the projector was drawn back, the 'hand' stretched and drew the arms of the crossbow away from the frame, increasing the torsion of the strands. The 'hand' was held down by a bolt which was then shot and the bowstring released. The mechanism was supported by a pillar with stays or struts. A *ballista* was capable of striking a target more than 350 metres distant.

Vitruvius provides directions on the 'tuning' of catapult strings, and on large-scale devices including the tortoise (*testudo*), a movable siege tower with a wooden parapet protected against fire used for direct assault on the enemy's walls and for cover during trench-work:

> Their fronts are made like the angles of triangles, so that when arrows are shot against them from a wall, they may receive the blows, not squarely in front, but glancing along the sides, and the men digging inside are protected without any risk. [10. 15. 1]

The only instance of the spring as part of the continuing operation of a machine appears in the water organ, which had a spring of elastic horn or metal to stop each note after the perforated slide sounding the note had been depressed.

When the keys are touched by the hands, they drive the sliders forward and draw them back regularly, alternately closing and opening holes; they produce resonant sounds in a great variety of melodies conforming to the laws of music. [10. 8. 6]

Ctesibius, the Alexandrian engineer of the third century, built the first water organ (*hydraulis*); the surviving example was found at Aquincum, near Budapest. Cicero, who describes the use of organs at banquets [*Tusc. Disp.* 3, 43], calls their sound a sensation as delectable to the ears as the most delicious fish to the palate! The organ was also used to accompany gladiatorial combats and circus performances.

Timechart

Building operations in Rome and Italy

46 BC	Julius Caesar	Forum Julium, Temple of Venus Genetrix dedicated.
44	Julius Caesar	Basilica Julia (incomplete).
42	L. Munatius Plancus	Temple of Saturn rebuilt.
39	C. Asinius Pollio	Atrium Libertatis rebuilt.
37	Agrippa, with L. Cocceius Auctus (archit.)	Portus Cumanus revived; Portus Julius completed; canal and tunnels (Cumae and Naples).
36	*Defeat of Sextus Pompey*	
	Cn. Domitius Calvinus	Regia rebuilt in marble.
34	T. Statilius Taurus	Rome's first stone amphitheatre begun. Temple of Apollo Medicus restored.
	C. Sosius	
33	Octavian	Porticus Metelli under repair.
	Agrippa (aedile), with Vitruvius (archit.) (?)	Hydraulic works and road repairs; builds Aqua Julia, repairs Aqua Appia, Aqua Marcia, and Anio Vetus.
	L. Marcius Philippus	Porticus Philippi; Temple of Hercules Musarum.
32	Octavian	Naval base at Misenum begun (?); Piscina Mirabilis at Bacoli (?); Theatre of Pompey repaired.
31	*Battle of Actium*	
30	T. Statilius Taurus	Stone amphitheatre dedicated.
29	Octavian's triple triumph	Temple of Deified Julius dedicated; Curia Julia, with Chalcidicum, dedicated; Rostra (Julian) inaugurated; Via Flaminia (to Rimini) under repair; 82 temples restored in Rome.
	Senate	The Actium Triumphal Arch, Forum Romanum.
	C. Cornelius Gallus (Octavian's *Praefectus fabrum*)	Forum Julium completed (?).

28	Octavian	Mausoleum begun. Temple of Apollo on the Palatine dedicated.
27	Augustus Vitruvius (archit.)	Via Flaminia repairs completed; Basilica at Fanum Fortunae (?).
27–24	*Augustus in Spain and Gaul*	
26	Agrippa	Saepta Julia dedicated.
25	Agrippa (consul III)	Pantheon completed; Baths of Agrippa (and Sudatorium) opened for public use.
24	Vitruvius	*Ten Books on Architecture* published (?).
23	Augustus	Porticus Octaviae (formerly Metelli) dedicated.
22	Augustus	Temple of Jupiter Tonans on the Capitoline.
22–19	*Augustus in Greece and Asia Minor*	
20	Augustus	Forum of Augustus; Temple of Mars the Avenger (completed 2 BC).
19	Agrippa	Golden Milestone erected (Forum Romanum); Aqua Virgo completed; Stagnum and Euripus (pool and ornamental water channel) completed.
	Senate	The Parthian Arch, Forum Romanum.
13	Augustus Senate	Theatre of Marcellus dedicated. Altar of Augustan Peace (completed 9 BC).

Glossary

adobe unburnt brick, dried in sun.

amphitheatre an oval area surrounded by tiers of seats for gladiatorial and hunting spectacles.

apse (adj. apsidal) semicircular recess, dome-roofed, especially at end of aisles.

aqueduct a pipeline designed to carry water.

ashlar masonry of squared stones laid horizontally with vertical joints.

atrium central hall of a Roman house comparable to a roofed patio with the central part of the roof (*compluvium*) left open to the sky to supply a catch-basin (*impluvium*) and cistern underneath.

basilica a rectangular building with a taller central area or nave with side aisles, used as covered forum and lawcourt building.

caryatid sculptured female figure used as columnar support for an entablature.

castrum a Roman military camp of square or rectangular design.

cella the central chamber or sanctuary of a temple.

chalcidicum a monumental porch or facade.

chorobates a wooden surveying instrument for siting and for determining land profiles.

cofferdam watertight enclosure constructed in water. The water is pumped out to permit labourers to work in a river or lake bed.

colonnade a row of columns, sometimes double, supporting a horizontal beam or roof.

dome (adj. domical) a rounded vault forming a roof.

entablature horizontal superstructure supported by a colonnade.

Forum an open square or market place serving religious, political, legal and social needs.

Horreum (pl. *horrea*) storage building, granary.

hypocaust floor with air space beneath for circulation of hot air (cf. radiant heating).

insula literally 'island', denoting a tenement building or apartment house, or a square or rectangular city block.

mortar a mixture of sand, lime and water used to combine stones and bricks.

oculus literally 'eye', a rounded opening or window in the roof of a bath building or temple (e.g. Pantheon).

opus caementicium concrete masonry of stones laid in mortar.

opus craticium wall construction using wooden framework or lattice work with careless mortar work and stucco facing, used chiefly in inferior housing and sub-standard tenements.

opus reticulatum 'network' (*reticulum* = 'fine net') facing of small squared blocks laid diagonally in concrete.

opus signinum waterproof concrete made with crushed brick.

peperino volcanic tufa from the Alban Hills, south-east of Rome.

peristyle inner garden of a house or villa surrounded by a colonnade (cf. cloister).

piscina literally 'fish pool', the plunge pool of a Roman bath.

porticus a colonnade attached to a building, often serving as porch.

pozzolana a volcanic ash mixed with regular mortar thereby enabling it to harden under water; so called from Puteoli (Pozzuoli) where it was first used.

reticulate see *opus reticulatum*.

specus literally 'cave', an aqueduct channel.

thermae literally 'heated rooms', denoting large public baths.

travertine grey stone containing lime quarried near Tibur (mod. Tivoli) and used extensively during late Republican and early Imperial times.

tufa building stone of Latium and Campania, consolidated volcanic dust and erupted material.

venter aqueduct channel across lower part of valleys with a low substructure to maintain level course of water to point where gradient changes; when the water reaches the upward slope, water in the pipes swells and flows uphill.

Select bibliography

Scholarly reference works, well illustrated

Boëthius, A. and Ward-Perkins, J. B. *Etruscan and Roman Architecture* Harmondsworth 1970

Liversidge, Joan *Britain in the Roman Empire* London 1968

Marsden, E. W. *Greek and Roman Artillery: Technical Treatises* Oxford 1971

McKay, A. G. *Houses, Villas and Palaces in the Roman World* Southampton 1975

Ward-Perkins, J. B. *Cities of Ancient Greece and Italy: Planning in Classical Antiquity* New York 1974

General studies, well illustrated

Grant, Michael *Cities of Vesuvius: Pompeii and Herculaneum* London 1972

Grant, Michael *The Roman Forum* London 1972

Sprague de Camp, L. *The Ancient Engineers* New York 1975 (paperback)

Wheeler, R. E. M. *Roman Art and Architecture* London 1974

For younger readers

Macaulay, David *City: A Story of Roman Planning and Construction* Boston 1974. Text and black and white drawings show how the Romans planned and constructed their cities for the people who lived in them.

Index